The ABC's
of
Bullying Prevention

by Dr. Kenneth Shore

DUDE PUBLISHING
A Division of
National Professional Resources, Inc.
Port Chester, New York

Cover/Book Design & Production by Andrea Cerone,
National Professional Resources, Inc., Port Chester, NY

Dude Publishing
A Division of National Professional Resources, Inc.
25 South Regent Street
Port Chester, New York 10573
Toll free: (800) 453-7461
Phone: (914) 937-8879

Visit our web site: www.NPRinc.com

Printed in the United States of America

ISBN 978-1-935609-39-1

In memory of
Arthur Schlosser

Table of Contents

Introduction

" If we are to reach real peace in the world, we shall have to begin with children." — **Mahatma Gandhi**

Bullying is a serious and pervasive problem in our schools. Various studies estimate that 15 to 20 percent of all students are victimized by bullies at some point in their school career. And, according to the National Youth Violence Prevention Resource Center, almost one in three children nationwide is involved in bullying, either as a bully or a victim.

Despite the prevalence of bullying and the severe consequences it can have for its victims as well as for those who are bystanders, schools frequently do not give it the attention it deserves. Bullying, however, is a problem that will not go away if ignored. Fortunately, schools have available to them a variety of strategies to prevent and/or decrease this problem. As with many problems within schools, it is more effective to prevent bullying than to wait for an incident to occur and then deal with it and the potential repercussions. Thus, any effort by schools to confront bullying must include a dual approach of not only taking steps to prevent bullying but also responding effectively to bullying incidents when they occur.

If schools are to make real advances in preventing incidents of bullying, these strategies need to be part of a school-wide anti-bullying campaign that has the commitment of staff, students and parents. A comprehensive, multifaceted, wide-ranging program that addresses the school climate and culture has the best chance of significantly reducing bullying in schools and making them safer for all children. A single assembly on bullying or an announcement by teachers that bullying is prohibited is simply not adequate to address the problem. In fact, research by Dan Olweus, as discussed in his 1993 book *Bullying at School,* indicates that schools can decrease bullying by as much as 50 percent with a comprehensive school-wide prevention program.

This book describes such a program, namely a comprehensive bullying prevention program that recognizes the need for both prevention and intervention components. It can be used on its own or as an accompaniment to a four-part DVD program also called *The ABC's of Bullying Prevention,* produced by the publisher of this book, National Professional Resources, Inc. This DVD training series was revised and reflects the most current practices and strategies in bullying prevention, including the latest information on cyberbullying as of this printing.

Each of the four (4) parts of the DVD targets a specific group that plays a key role in responding to and preventing bullying. There is a component for administrators and pupil services staff (which includes guidance counselors, psychologists, nurses and social workers), one for teachers, one for paraprofessionals, and one for parents. This book is organized in a parallel format, with a chapter devoted to each of these groups. In terms of writing style, I have chosen to use he when referring to a student although it is recognized that a sizeable number of children involved in bullying either as bullies or victims are female. Also for ease of reading, I have chosen to use the pronoun she when referring to teachers, though in no way is this meant to exclude all the terrific male teachers in today's school.

While the four segments contain some common material about bullying, each one also presents information specific to the target group, including strategies they can use to prevent incidents as well as challenges that each group faces in dealing with bullying. These staff development videos/DVDs can be shown at faculty meetings, school safety committee meetings, PTA meetings and community-wide meetings. They are intended to stimulate discussion about the problem of bullying and hopefully motivate the school and community as a whole to take comprehensive measures to deal with the problem.

A bullying prevention program is most effective when implemented at the district level, with support of the Board as well as administration. However, it can also be implemented on a single school or even a classroom level. This book examines ways that bullying prevention procedures can be employed at the building and classroom levels. Even if a school opts not to implement a bullying prevention program throughout the entire building, teachers can still use the practices described in this book to confront the problem of bullying within their class.

This book goes into depth on a variety of topics that are also referred to in the videos/DVDs. In Chapter 3 it describes in detail 12 key elements of a bullying prevention program, a more comprehensive presentation than is presented in the media format. In subsequent chapters the book examines what each group can do to deal with the problem of bullying. The reader should be able to gain an understanding of the basic issues of bullying, the bullying prevention program and their role in dealing with this problem by reading Chapters 1 and 3 as well as the chapter that specifically applies to them. This material thus provides school staff with the information they need to implement a school-wide bullying prevention program while the video/DVD components provide schools with an effective tool for raising awareness about bullying and motivating school staff to implement a prevention program.

For those who wish more information about bullying, Chapter 9 offers an extensive list of resources. Some of the books listed focus on the specific problem of bullying while others deal with the challenges of creating a more peaceful classroom or helping a child learn to develop effective social skills. This chapter also provides a list of books for children that teachers might use in the classroom or parents might read to their children. Lists of videos, web sites and organizations that offer additional information on the topic of bullying are also included.

Bullying prevention may also be seen as part of the overall effort of the schools to assist in the social emotional/ moral development of each child. As such it is closely aligned to other significant initiatives, most specifically Character Education and social emotional learning. It certainly reinforces efforts directed at growth in school civility.

Acknowledgments

I want to acknowledge a number of people who made key contributions to this book as well as the companion video project. Dr. Robert Hanson, president of National Professional Resources, Inc. recognized the importance of the issue of bullying and the critical need for staff development in this area. He was a continual source of support and ideas during the entire project. Dr. Joseph Casbarro employed his keen understanding of school culture, his creative intelligence and his technical expertise to develop a powerful set of videos. The manuscript was vastly improved by the sharp eye and insightful ideas of Helene Hanson. And Andrea Cerone deserves recognition for her reader-friendly book design.

Chapter 1
Bullying: An Overview

Most adults can probably recall incidents of bullying from their own schooldays. This is not surprising since bullying is a problem that has been with us since the advent of schools. And for a significant number of these adults, their recollections bring to mind a time when they were the target of the bullying. They often recall these incidents in vivid detail because they were so hurtful that they left a permanent imprint in their memories.

While bullying is a problem that has been with us since time immemorial, it appears to have become even more serious and more pervasive in recent years, exacting a terrible toll on many students. Clearly it is a problem that schools must recognize and address. After all, the first and foremost obligation of any school is to provide a safe and secure environment where teachers can teach and students can learn.

In this chapter we will take a look at some of the basic issues involving bullying. We will examine what bullying is, and is not, we will discuss the many shapes and forms that bullying can take, and we will consider the consequences that bullying can have not only for the victim but also for the bully and the bystander. We will also look at why bullying does not always come to the attention of school staff, and review some of the myths surrounding bullying that may keep adults from taking it seriously. And finally we will profile the bully, victim, and bystander to better understand why they may assume these roles.

What Do We Mean by Bullying

Bullying typically takes place when a stronger or more powerful child intentionally and repeatedly hurts, threatens or torments a more vulnerable child. There are thus three distinguishing features of bullying: it is deliberate/intentional, it happens more than once, and there is a marked imbalance of power between the bully and the victim. In short, bullying is a one-sided, unfair match.

Bullying is thus different from a single incident of teasing. It also differs from play. It is, in fact, an abuse of power. In addition, it is distinct from the normal conflicts of childhood. It is not bullying when two children of approximately equal strength or power are engaged in a fight. Thus, while all acts of bullying are aggressive, not all aggressive acts are bullying.

Bullying can occur face to face or it can happen behind one's back. Bullying can be short-term or it can last a long time. Bullying can be done by an individual or by a group. And while bullies are more likely to be male, we are seeing an increasing number of girls who are bullying their classmates. The type of bullying done by girls, however, often differs from that done by boys. Boys are more likely to attack their peers verbally or physically while girls are more likely to bully indirectly, by using relational methods.

For example, they might exclude their victims from activities, convince others to reject them or spread rumors about them. Bullying by girls can often take the form of mean-spirited backbiting and gossiping.

Bullying can start in elementary school, usually reaches its peak in middle school and gradually declines in high school. By high school, bullies and victims are often pursuing different interests and subjects so their paths are less likely to cross than in middle school. At the high school level, bullying is more likely to take the form of harassment, often sexual in nature. And bullying may take place in any part of the school building, but it is most common in areas that have minimal supervision. Bullies may extort lunch money from their classmates in the lunchroom, jostle them in the hallway, hit them in the locker room or exclude them from playing games on the playground. It is important to attempt to identify what bullying feels like, looks like, and sounds like.

The Many Forms of Bullying

When we think of bullying, we usually think of a child being physically aggressive towards another child. But bullying can take many shapes and forms. In addition to being physical, it can also be verbal and psychological in nature, as the list below indicates. Bullies may:
- taunt, put-down, or ridicule their peers on an ongoing basis
- make offensive comments to other children based on their race, gender, religion or disability
- write nasty, hurtful things about classmates
- intimidate, terrorize or threaten other children

- send offensive or threatening messages to others through the use of their computer or cell phone (called "cyberbullying")
- spread rumors about other children
- play mean practical jokes on peers
- get other children in trouble
- intentionally exclude or leave other children out of activities
- persuade their peers to reject or shun other children
- make other children do things they do not want to do
- take or damage other children's belongings
- force children to hand over their money or their possessions, as a form of extortion
- have unwanted physical contact with girls
- hit, push, trip, kick or pinch other children

In recent years a new form of bullying has emerged called cyberbullying. Using their computer or cell phone, children may harass or torment their peers in a variety of ways. They may send offensive or threatening messages to peers; they may post humiliating pictures of classmates on the Internet; they may conduct online polls to identify the ugliest classmate; they may create web sites to ridicule other children. These messages may be sent by e-mail, by instant message, or by text message.

This remote form of bullying allows children to use the anonymity of the Internet to cause anguish to their victims without seeing its effects. While these incidents may originate at home, they often find their way into school, sometimes giving rise to conflicts that require intervention by school staff. In some schools the problem has become so disruptive that staff have found it necessary to hold assemblies to discuss cyberbullying.

What are the Effects of Bullying

Being taunted or attacked physically can be one of the most painful experiences of childhood and can leave lasting psychological scars. In some cases it can have life-long consequences. Victims of bullying may experience anxiety, low self-esteem, depression and in some cases even suicidal thoughts. They may come to view school, where most incidents of bullying take place, as an unsafe, anxiety-provoking environment and may be afraid of attending. Some may even refuse to go to school rather than face the ordeal of bullying. In fact, a study by the National Association of School Psychologists estimates that 160,000 children miss school every day for fear of being bullied.

Bullying also affects the students who witness the incidents. It can give rise to a climate of fear and anxiety in school, distracting students from their schoolwork and impeding their ability to learn. According to a recent study, about ten percent of students are afraid during much of the school day. Students who witness their classmates being victimized wonder, "Am I going to be next?" The possibility of being bullied may cause these bystanders to live in a state of fear and focus on little else. This is hardly surprising when you consider that children surveyed rated bullying the worst experience of childhood, other than the death of a loved one. Witnesses to bullying may also suffer pangs of guilt that they did nothing to stop the attack on their classmate.

These are some of the short-term effects of bullying. As we shall see later in this chapter, bullying can have long-term effects as well.

Bullying: A Hidden Problem

Despite the widespread and serious nature of bullying, schools do not always give this problem the attention it deserves. Some school staff may not act upon hearing reports of bullying because they may not perceive it as serious. Evidence for this comes from a 1999 article by Kenneth Schroeder in Education Digest which reported that 71 percent of teachers or other adults in the classroom ignored bullying incidents.

There are a number of reasons why school staff do not respond consistently to incidents of bullying. First, adults may not always consider these incidents as serious problems worthy of a response. They may take the view that these incidents are a normal part of growing up and that students have to learn to stand up for themselves. This is just one of many myths that may keep adults from responding seriously to bullying. Other myths about bullying are described later in this chapter.

A second reason that school staff may not respond to bullying is that they may be unaware that it is taking place. Bullies are often very adept at harassing their classmates outside the presence of adults. In addition, surveys indicate that victims often fail to report bullying to adults because they are not confident that their concerns will be taken seriously or that steps will be taken to curb the problem. Students may also keep bullying incidents to themselves because of shame about what happened or fear of retaliation. It is not surprising then that on surveys children report a much higher frequency of bullying in school than teachers report.

Classmates who witness bullying also often fail to report it. They are reluctant to break the "code of silence" and tell on a student, perhaps fearing that the bully will target them next. This passivity of the bystanders only serves to empower the bully and further isolate the victim.

Because of a combination of these factors, bullying incidents often go undetected by adults. The failure of adults to acknowledge many bullying incidents or consistently respond when they do become aware sends the message to bullies that they can get away with what they are doing. When adults ignore bullying incidents, bullies come to believe that their behavior is acceptable.

Members of the school community must send a very different message, namely that they will be vigilant in looking out for bullying and respond seriously when it is detected. Students need firm rules and assurance that adults are in charge, and willing and able to enforce the rules. Bullying is thus a problem that schools must confront head-on, not only to protect the victims of bullying but also to send a strong message that bullying will not be tolerated and that measures will be taken to ensure that all students are safe and protected. Fortunately bullying is a problem about which something can be done, if administrators, school staff and parents place the safety and security of children at the top of their priority list.

Ten Myths About Bullying

As introduced earlier in this book, people may make false or misleading claims about bullying. These erroneous beliefs or myths serve to downplay the seriousness of bullying and may keep school staff from taking the necessary action. Confronting these false beliefs about bullying may help to change their response to the problem. Let's take a look at a number of these myths.

"Bullying builds character."

Rather than building character, however, bullying can cause children to be anxious, fearful and unhappy. It may also lower their self-esteem. They may come to believe that something is wrong with them and that they even deserved the treatment. Some adults may even erroneously contend that bullying can be a learning experience, but for most victims the lesson of bullying is that the world is unsafe and people are not to be trusted.

"Bullying is a harmless rite of passage that is a natural part of growing up."

Bullying may be a fact of life for many children but this does not mean that it needs to be accepted as a normal or inevitable part of childhood. And it is certainly not harmless. Many bullying victims endure lasting psychological scars.

"Bullying is no more than kids being kids."

Bullying is far different from child's play. When children fool around, they do so out of choice. But victims of bullying do not choose to be tormented. And bullies and victims are not on an equal footing. The bully is typically stronger and more physically imposing than the victim, or in some other way has more power.

"Kids bounce back quickly after being bullied."

While some children weather bullying more easily than others, many suffer long-term pain from the experience. And those who insist that they survived the ordeal without harm may have forgotten the genuine hurt that they felt at the time.

"Victims of bullying usually bring it on themselves through their behavior."

According to this notion, the victim provokes the bully into reacting and is thus blameworthy. The reality is that bullies often choose their victims because they appear weak, isolated or vulnerable or because they seem different in some way. We thus need to convey the message to victims that they did nothing wrong and it is the bullies who are in the wrong.

"Bullying will disappear if you ignore it."

In fact, the opposite is the case. Closing your eyes to the problem is giving license to bullies to continue inflicting pain on other children and telling victims that they have to handle bullying on their own. One student, when asked why he was bullying another student, gave the simple answer "because I can." He was bullying because he felt he could get away with it. The reality is that bullying must be confronted vigorously and bullies must be held accountable for their behavior.

"Sticks and stones may break my bones but names can never hurt me."

Suggesting that a victim say this to a bully will likely provide little comfort to a child who is being constantly teased or called names. The pain caused by these verbal blows can often last longer than those from physical blows, especially if they are frequent and ongoing. This is captured in the following poem by an unknown author:

Sticks and stones may break my bones,
But words can also hurt me.
Sticks and stones break only skin,
While words are ghosts that haunt me.

Slant and curved the word-swords fall
To pierce and stick inside me.
Bats and bricks may ache through bones,
But words can mortify me.

Pain from words has left its scar
On mind and heart that's tender.
Cuts and bruises now have healed;
It's words that I remember.

"Victims of bullying must learn to stand up for themselves."

While we want children to learn to resolve conflicts with their peers on their own, this does not mean that they should be left to fend for themselves in the face of typically bigger, stronger children. Some students are simply unequipped to deal with this intimidation so that retaliation could result in their getting hurt. In these cases, they need the help of an adult. And it needs to be explained to the victims of bullying that seeking help is not a sign of weakness but rather a sign of good sense.

"Hit the bully back and he'll leave you alone."

Not only is this untrue in most cases, but it is likely to make the problem worse. Bullies are unlikely to back down if their victims fight back. Rather, they are likely to strike out if challenged, placing the victim in harm's way. This approach can also give the message that violence is acceptable, and retaliation a way to solve problems.

"No students are bullied in this school."

While some principals would like you to think that bullying does not take place in their schools, the reality is that virtually every school has bullies. Principals would therefore be prudent to embrace a bullying prevention program such as the one provided in this book and the media series. It is an excellent resource as it enables them to focus on proven strategies for prevention as well as skills that must be used in intervention and is thus a powerful example of a balanced proactive and reactive approach.

Recognizing the Signs of Bullying

As discussed previously, school staff may not respond to bullying because they may not always know when it occurs. There are two primary reasons for this. First, bullies are more likely to harass other children when adults are not present. Most bullying incidents take place in areas with minimal adult supervision such as the playground, rest room, locker room, cafeteria and hallway. Second, victims of bullying often fail to inform school staff of bullying incidents because they are not confident that staff will take appropriate action. Victims may also suffer in silence because they are ashamed of what happened or fear retaliation from the bully. As a result, bullying is a problem that often goes unrecognized by school staff.

Because of these obstacles to the detection of bullying, it is critical that school staff be on the lookout for signs that a student has been bullied. While the actual incident may not be observed, the results of the bullying are most often seen in the behavior of the victim. The following warning signs may suggest that a student has been the target of bullying:

- many school absences
- anxiety during class
- unusual sadness
- isolation from peers
- clingy behavior
- a decline in academic performance
- avoidance of certain school areas
- frequent visits to the school nurse
- change in eating patterns

Of course, the more of these signs that a student exhibits, the more reason to suspect that he is being bullied.

The Bully

Bullies are typically bigger and stronger than their classmates. They are generally of average intelligence although their school performance is often below average. They often have a history of aggressive behavior dating back to early elementary school. Their quickness to anger may be fueled by their social misperceptions. They may view the world as a threatening place and often perceive hostility where none is present. They can be very reactive to social slights and may lash out at classmates with little provocation, sometimes because they see no alternative to aggression. They often feel no sense of remorse at hurting other children and show them little sympathy. This lack of empathy may be one of the most critical elements in the picture of a bully. This absence of empathy is frequently compounded by a lack of self-control as well as lack of conscience.

Children may bully for a variety of reasons. Some may torment their classmates to gain a sense of power and control over them. Some may bully in an effort to gain recognition and status from peers, something that they may not be able to get in other ways. Others may bully in an effort to compensate for their feelings of inadequacy. Still others may target their classmates as a way of venting frustration with problems at home or problems in school (for example, learning problems or peer rejection). And some may bully as a result of having been bullied themselves.

Bullies usually choose as targets peers who are weak, or less popular, and unlikely to resist. They may zero in on children who stand out in some way such as the teacher's pet, a child with a speech defect, a slow learner, a child with big ears, a child who wears the "wrong" clothes or an English Language Learner.

Bullies are not born, they are made, which means they can be unmade. They are often taught from an early age that the way to get what they want is through force. They may learn to respond to challenges with confrontation and to express themselves with their fists rather than words. As they get older, they are at risk for further acts of violence, including frequent fighting and carrying of weapons.

Bullies' education in aggression may begin at home, particularly if they come from households where there is little parental supervision, and a lack of warmth and attention. Their parents may model aggressive behavior as a way of solving problems. They may discipline through a combination of angry outbursts and corporal punishment. The message their children receive is that "might makes right." Such parents may support their child's bullying behavior towards peers by their failure to disapprove of it, or their outright endorsement of it. In addition, the parents may fail to model non-violent ways of dealing with social problems so that their children may not learn the social skills needed to resolve conflicts through cooperative means.

Children also learn aggressive behavior from the media, notably television. The amount of violence they are exposed to on television is simply astounding. By the age of 14, a child will have seen as many as 11,000 murders on television. Even the average cartoon has 26 violent incidents. Children may see television characters who get their way, settle disputes and acquire things by using force without suffering any negative consequences. The lesson they learn is that aggression pays off. Research indicates that children who see violence frequently on television may become less sensitive to the pain and suffering of others and may view aggression as an acceptable way of solving problems.

School bullies often face problems as they grow into adulthood. They are more likely than their peers to drop out of school, have difficulty holding jobs, have problems sustaining relationships, be abusive of their spouses, and have aggressive children. And they are more prone to criminal behavior. One study initiated by Leonard Eron in 1963 followed individuals over a 22-year period and found that children who were aggressive to their peers at age eight were five times more likely than their non-aggressive peers to have a criminal record (usually antisocial offenses) by the age of 30.

A particularly alarming pattern is that aggressive children often grow up to be harsh, punitive parents who have children who become bullies themselves. In short, children of bullies often become bullies. The challenge for those working with aggressive children and their families is to try to disrupt this cycle of violence.

The Victim

Bullies typically target children who are vulnerable in some way. The victims of bullying tend to be shy, sensitive, and insecure. Some typically have low self-esteem and may even come to believe that they deserved the treatment they received from the bully. While they tend to be withdrawn from their peers, they may stand out in some way; they may be shorter or heavier than their peers, they may come from a different background than most of their classmates, they may have an accent, or they may have a physical disability.

Victims also tend to be loners who have few friends in school and low social status. They typically have poor social and communication skills, making it difficult for them to deflect taunting or resolve conflicts in a cooperative manner. Because of their isolation from peers, classmates are less likely to rally to their defense when they are bullied. Often overprotected by their parents, victims frequently lack independence and assertiveness. They are usually weaker than their tormentors and thus have difficulty defending themselves.

While many victims of bullying are passive and withdrawn, some can be provocative in nature. They may act in an annoying manner with their classmates and get on the nerves of the bully. The bully may justify his aggressive behavior towards the student by claiming that "he deserved it", even though he passed up more reasonable ways of dealing with the problem.

Students react to being bullied in various ways. Some may try to project a tough facade in an effort to convince peers that the bully's behavior had little effect on them. Some may vent their frustration by retaliating against the bully physically or calling him names. And some may react by becoming bullies themselves. Indeed, many youngsters implicated in school shootings have a history of being victimized by bullies.

Some victims may have severe emotional reactions to bullying. In the short term, they may dissolve in tears but over the longer term they may be observed withdrawing from their peers. Their academic performance may decline as a result of difficulty focusing on schoolwork. They may go through school in a constant state of fear, avoiding unsupervised areas and activities where bullying is likely to occur. They may change their route to school in an effort to avoid meeting up with their tormentor. In extreme cases, they may resist coming to school. They may even develop stomachaches or headaches from the pressures of being bullied. Their problems may persist into adulthood. Victims of bullying are more likely to suffer from depression and low self-esteem during their adult years.

The Bystander

To fully understand the problem of bullying, it is important to consider the students who observe the bullying — the bystanders. Fearful of incurring the wrath of the bully, they may repress their feelings of empathy for the victim and opt to stay on the sidelines. Their failure to respond, however, may only strengthen the bully's impulse to continue his behavior. For a school to be effective in confronting the problem of bullying, it must activate the bystanders and convert them from a silent majority into a caring and vocal majority. As will be seen in Chapter 3, this is one of the keys to an effective bullying prevention program.

Chapter 2
Cyberbullying

QUESTION: What do the following incidents have in common?

- A middle-school girl breaks into a classmate's e-mail account and sends rude messages from that e-mail address to make it appear that the classmate is harassing others.

- An eleventh-grade boy who is angry after being jilted by a girl inserts her face on a pornographic picture using photo-editing tools and then posts it in a blog for others to see.

- Middle-school students vote for the most unpopular student in school on the Internet.

- An eighth-grade boy uses his cell phone camera to take a picture of a classmate getting undressed in the locker room and uploads it to a web site for viewing by other students.

- A group of middle-school girls cast votes online by "instant messaging" for a student to be excluded from their table during lunch.

- A girl dislikes a classmate so she arranges for her friends to remove their friendship links on the classmate's social networking profile.
- A tenth-grade boy, while talking online, deceives a girl into revealing sensitive information about herself and then forwards that information to others via text messages.
- A teenage girl spreads nasty rumors about a classmate in her online blog.
- A twelfth-grade boy posts personal information about girls, including sexual experiences, on a web site accessible to classmates.
- A fifth-grade boy sends hurtful e-mails to other students without identifying himself.
- A 13-year old girl sends a semi-nude picture of herself to a boy she hopes to date. The picture is sent to classmates, via cell phone, leading to relentless and nasty name-calling. A few weeks after entering eighth grade, she takes her life.

ANSWER: They are all examples of cyberbullying. And they all have actually happened!

What is Cyberbullying?

Cyberbullying is a fast-growing form of bullying that has emerged with the advent of technology. It involves sending offensive, humiliating or threatening messages or images through the computer or cell phone. It is most often seen with middle- and high-school students although elementary-school students as young as eight- or nine-years old have also engaged in this high-tech form of bullying as well as been its victims. Similar to face-to-face bullying, cyberbullying tends to decrease as students enter upper high school grades and become more mature in their social interactions.

Cyberbullying is limited to interactions between children or adolescents. If an adult is involved, it is typically called cyberstalking or harassment. In addition, it is not considered cyberbullying but rather sexual exploitation when an adult tries to lure a child he or she has met online into a face-to-face meeting.

Cyberbullying may take various forms, ranging from a cruel joke to a vicious threat. The most common form of cyberbullying is the posting of hurtful comments and rumors. Some engage in this harassing behavior in an effort to gain attention and approval from peers. Others may be trying to avenge a perceived slight. And still others may be seeking entertainment and an escape from boredom.

Cyberbullying is often triggered by difficulties in personal relationships. As an example, a boy who has been hurt by a former girlfriend, may take his revenge on the Internet. He may post disparaging comments or even display inappropriate images of her online. Cyberbullying may also be a vehicle for expressing a person's prejudice, as evidenced by offensive comments made online about another's race, religion, physical appearance or sexual orientation.

Both boys and girls engage in cyberbullying although their methods of choice often differ. Girls are more likely to post rumors or offensive messages about others while boys are more likely to post compromising pictures and videos of others and hack into their computer systems and steal their passwords.

Cyberbullying may be perpetrated by someone the victim knows or by a complete stranger. In some cases cyberbullies have been victims of face-to-face bullying and are using the Internet to fight back in an arena where they feel more comfortable. They may not be as physically imposing as their tormentors but they are often formidable online adversaries because of their technological know-how. The same child or teen may thus be a victim one moment and a cyberbully the next. Cyberbullies may also enlist others who may or may not know the victim to participate in the harassment. This is cyberbullying by proxy and can result in many individuals attacking the victim.

Prevalence of Cyberbullying

Cyberbullying has increased dramatically in recent years to the extent that it is now a serious concern among parents, school principals and law enforcement officials. While estimates of the prevalence of cyberbullying vary based on the age group studied and the definition of cyberbullying, there is no question that it is a pervasive problem among children and teens.

According to a study of cyberbullying by researchers Sameer Hinduja and Justin W. Patchin, *Bullying Beyond the Schoolyard: Preventing and Responding to Cyberbullying* (Corwin Press, 2008) about 20 percent of youth who participated in the study indicated they had been victims of online bullying. Other studies have provided even stronger evidenced of the widespread nature of cyberbullying. A 2004 study by i-SAFE America of 1500 students of fourth to eighth grade age found that more than half had been affected by cyberbullying. In particular, the survey found that 58 percent of students received offensive comments while online while 53 percent acknowledged having posted negative comments to another person. Of particular concern from this study was a finding that 35 percent of students had been threatened while on the Internet.

The Digital World of Our Children

The pervasiveness of cyberbullying is due in large part to the wide-scale use of the Internet and cell phones by children and teens. Often the first thing they do when they get home from school is to log on to the Internet, often going on social networking sites such as Facebook and My Space. They use the computer and cell phone to talk with their friends, to develop new relationships, and to obtain and convey information.

For many children these technologies are their social lifeline. Their online activity extends well beyond sending e-mails. They may send instant messages (IM's), post information about themselves or others in blogs, talk to others in chat rooms, interact with others on social networking sites, play online games, and even develop their own web sites. Cell phones, with their capacity for sending text messages and taking and sending pictures and videos, have only increased the high-tech communication options. Three out of four teens have cell phones and most use them more for texting than for talking. The average teenager sends more than six text messages every waking hour. Girls are especially prolific texters, sending more than eight per waking hour.

Social networking sites are widely used by children and teenagers. While Facebook and MySpace, the most common of these sites, require users to be at least 13 years old, many children younger than 13 gain access to these sites by pretending to be older when they sign up. A recent study by the Kaiser Family Foundation found that

75 percent of 7th through 12th graders surveyed reported they had a profile on a social networking site. Children as young as five have their choice of a range of social networking sites they can join that place an emphasis on safety and age-appropriateness.

While these technologies open up a world of information as well as connections to people all over the globe, they also have their pitfalls. In particular, young people face the risk of invasion of their privacy. Every time children or teenagers complete a profile on a social networking site such as Facebook, post a comment online, send a picture of themselves to a friend, text an intimate message to a boyfriend or girlfriend, they run the risk of this information being disclosed to a vast invisible, anonymous audience.

Cyberbullying: The Anonymity Factor

Cyberbullying can be done anytime, anywhere and by anyone with Internet access. It does not require the presence of its victim; it only requires access to a computer or cell phone. Hiding behind a mask of anonymity, cyberbullies can thus invade a victim's home without ever entering the door. Students who have been victims of cyberbullying describe a feeling of being trapped because they cannot escape the taunts of the bully. Even the targets of face-to-face bullying can find safe haven in their homes; not so for the victims of cyberbullying. And the cyberbullying can go on 24 hours a day, seven days a week.

The anonymity of the Internet serves to embolden cyberbullies. Using web sites or screen names that are difficult to trace, they may feel like they can strike out at others invisibly with little chance of being caught. They may feel freer to say things about people online than they would say to their face. As one teenager stated: "I can say what I feel to a kid I don't like without him knowing who said it, so I don't have to deal with his reaction."

By being removed from their targets and thus not seeing the impact of their actions, cyberbullies can delude themselves into thinking they have not really hurt anybody. As a result, they are unlikely to feel a sense of empathy or remorse for their victims.

Similarly cyberbullies, believing that they are invisible to their victims as well as adults, may feel that they are immune from detection and thus not subject to retaliation or discipline. As many learn, this is often not the case: many cyberbullies can be detected because they leave digital evidence of their actions that can be used to identify them as the source.

At the same time cyberbullying suffers from one of the same obstacles to detection as face-to-face bullying: children and teens are often reluctant to report it to an adult. There is a tacit understanding that "what occurs online stays online." Children may fear that if they report disturbing online incidents to their parents they will be barred from using the Internet or may be subject to further attacks if the cyberbully learns they have told an adult. As a result, parents and teachers are often the last to know about incidents of cyberbullying.

Impact of Cyberbullying

Because of the unique features of the Internet and its widespread use, cyberbullying can be devastating to its victims, perhaps more so than face-to-face bullying. Information about someone can be captured easily online and sent via the computer in a matter of seconds to potentially millions of people with the mere click of a mouse. And once the information is sent, it is typically irretrievable.

Even though victims of cyberbullying may not know the individuals who are targeting them, the emotional harm can be just as profound as that from traditional bullying. The attack may be anonymous, but the hurt is no less real. The attack may consist of words only, but the impact is no less painful than many physical attacks. Indeed, the effects of cyberbullying can be overwhelming and long-term.

Victims of cyberbullying have experienced some of the same problems experienced by those who have experienced face-to-face bullying, including humiliation, low self-esteem, anger and depression. These emotional problems may in turn give rise to other difficulties, including poor school performance, school avoidance, social withdrawal, anti-social acts and self-destructive behavior. In extreme cases, the feelings of desperation that can accompany bullying in general and cyberbullying in particular have led some victims to take their own lives. This problem has received so much attention in the media that the term 'bullycide' has been developed to describe this behavior.

Forms of Cyberbullying

Bullying in cyberspace may assume various forms. Indeed, the ways that cyberbullies can torment their victims are limited only by their imagination and technological savvy. The Center for Safe and Responsible Internet Use has identified the following types of cyberbullying on its web site www.cyberbully.org:

- **Flaming**: Sending an angry or confrontational message on the Internet in an effort to upset someone or inflame a situation.

- **Online Harassment**: Repeatedly sending nasty, disparaging messages by e-mail, instant messages, bulletin board postings or while in a chat room.

- **Cyberstalking**: Harassing someone online by sending threatening or intimidating messages or making unwanted advances.

- **Denigration**: Making offensive, hurtful or untrue statements about a person for others to see online. This includes posting rumors to hurt others' reputation.

- **Masquerading**: Pretending to be another person and sending/posting offensive information online that places that person in a vulnerable/embarrassing situation or damages his/her reputation.

- **Outing**: Sending or posting sensitive or embarrassing information about a person online, including forwarding private messages or pictures.

- **Trickery**: Deceiving a person into disclosing private information that is then placed online for public viewing.

- **Exclusion**: Intentionally excluding a person from an online group such as an IM "buddies" list or a game.

Another very disturbing trend that has emerged in recent years is called sexting. This involves individuals sending sexually-related pictures or videos to others, typically through cell phones. These are often sent to boys or girls in whom they have a romantic interest.

This is more common than might be thought. The National Campaign to Prevent Teen and Unplanned Pregnancy conducted a study in 2008 and found that 20 percent of teens had sent or posted nude or semi-nude images of themselves through the cell phone or computer. This can become cyberbullying when these pictures are then sent by the recipient to other individuals. In extreme cases, this can give rise to blackmail or extortion. Sexting has become such a concern that 21 states have introduced or passed laws related to this problem.

A Glossary of Terms

In order to better understand the nature of cyberbullying, it is helpful to become familiar with some of the computer-related terms that may be encountered in dealing with this problem. In addition to the terms provided in the previous section, Forms of Cyberbullying, the following are presented:

Acceptable Use Policy (AUP): A set of rules developed by a network or web site that defines the ways in which the network or web site can be used. It typically defines in precise terms what users are allowed, and not allowed, to do. Most schools have specific policies to address this.

Anonymizer: An intermediary that allows an Internet user to hide his/her online address. This enables the user to engage in online activities without being able to be traced.

Bash Board: An online bulletin board or chat room where users can post anonymous comments, typically of an offensive or malicious nature, about others for public viewing.

Blocking: Denying certain individuals access to specific sites on the Internet.

Blog: An online and publicly accessible diary in which users often provide personal information about themselves or others. The writer of a blog is called a blogger and the process of writing it is called blogging. Cyberbullying may occur through the posting of hateful or nasty comments on a blog.

Buddy List: A list of individuals (usually screen names) a person communicates with online on a regular basis; it can be accessed easily by computer.

Bulletin Board: An online forum where individuals can exchange ideas and information about various topics. All postings can be seen by visitors to the board.

Bully Blog: An online journal intended to ridicule, embarrass or threaten others.

Bullycide: Suicide that is the result of relentless bullying.

Chat: An online conversation in a chat room (see below) engaged in by people who use screen names rather than their real names.

Chat Room: An online meeting place where individuals can talk with others in "real time" so that their comments are seen almost instantly. Chat rooms require caution because you are never sure who is talking with you or reading your messages.

Cyberthreat: Online message in which a person threatens directly or indirectly to hurt someone else or himself. An online threat to hurt someone else may constitute a criminal act punishable by law.

Digital Footprint: Electronic traces of an individual's use of the Internet.

Filtering Software: Software that prevents access to certain information on the Internet based on pre-selected criteria. Also called content-control software.

Instant Messaging (IM): An online communication system allowing users to talk with each other privately by sending messages back and forth. IMs are often used in chat rooms by users who wish to have a private conversation.

Internet Service Provider (ISP): A company/organization that provides residences or companies with an Internet connection. An ISP can be helpful in identifying someone who has engaged in cyberbullying.

Monitoring: The process of recording Internet activity through the use of computer software.

Netiquette: Short for "Internet etiquette," this is a set of informal rules of courtesy that individuals are expected to use when communicating online.

Online Slam Book: Similar to a slam book where students pass around a notebook that asks questions that can sometimes be humiliating or hurtful to others, the Internet version allows youngsters to post answers online to questions on a web site or threaded discussion. These questions are often offensive (for example, "Who is the ugliest girl in school?") and responses can be seen by online visitors.

Privacy Policy: Policy that guides how web sites deal with personal information received from users. It is usually contained on the site and typically describes what information is collected, how it will be used, and with whom it will be shared.

The Parent's Role

Just as with the more traditional form of bullying, parents and school staff must be proactive in preventing cyberbullying as well as dealing with incidents when they do occur. The primary goal is for adults to help children and teens learn to act in a safe and respectful manner while online. Similarly, they need to help youngsters respond to cyberbullying in ways that both prevent its escalation and confront its more threatening forms. Adults may lack the technological savvy of their children but they can certainly teach them how to make good decisions and exercise sound judgment when it comes to interacting with others online. Without adult guidance, cyberbullying is likely to continue unabated.

The surest way to protect your children as they send and receive messages online is to be with them and help them learn to interact online in a responsible way. But that is not always feasible—nor is it always desirable. Just as you convey to your children rules for dealing with strangers, it is also important that you set out some guidelines for how they use the Internet and cell phones. While your children may protest that what they say and do online is their business, you have an obligation to ensure that they are engaged in responsible online behavior and are not harassing or being harassed by others. The following pages describe steps parents can take to lessen their children's exposure to online social cruelty as well as deal with incidents when they happen.

Parent Strategies for Preventing Cyberbullying

Consider not allowing your elementary-school child to go on the Internet if you are not home. Time-limiting software may enable you to do this.

Place the computer in a common area. Select a location in your home such as the family room, living room or the kitchen. In this way, you can keep an eye on whom they are talking with and what sites they are visiting.

Set some guidelines for your children's Internet use. By sitting with them when they are on the computer, you can gain helpful information to establish some sensible online rules. Consider putting them in writing and posting them near the computer. These guidelines might include the amount of time they can use the computer, the topics they are barred from discussing online, the messages they receive that they should bring to your attention, and the appropriate response to requests for personal information.

Teach your children Internet etiquette (netiquette). Emphasize the importance of communicating in a polite, respectful manner when on the Internet. Let them know that you expect them to treat others on the Internet the way they would want to be treated. Also convey that they should not say to someone on the computer or through a text what they wouldn't say to them in person. If warranted, make it clear that sending hurtful or threatening messages to anyone online is unacceptable and will result in a loss of computer privileges. See page 43 of this chapter entitled Technology Do's and Don't's for Children and Teens for specific tips to discuss with your children to lessen their chance of being cyberbullied or becoming a cyberbully.

Explain why they should not post personal information online. Your children may not understand that personal information posted on the Internet will allow people they meet online to contact them – and not always for appropriate reasons. Tell them specifically what information should not be posted online, including name, screen name, street address, e-mail address, and telephone number, or any similar information about members of their families or their friends.

Get to know your children's Internet friends. This will help you monitor their online influences. If they use AOL, they will likely have a buddy list of individuals they communicate with regularly and can access easily by computer. Talk with your children about what other sites they visit and who else they talk to online.

Monitor the chat rooms that your children enter. This could be done by sitting with them as they talk with others. Children may receive offensive comments or threats in these areas. Encourage them to go into chat rooms where they can talk with friends or family members or rooms that are hosted by responsible adults.

Review your children's Internet activity by checking the browser history. The browser history will indicate what sites they have visited (unless they have erased it). Have a talk with them if they are going to sites that concern you.

Consider using filtering software on your computer. This software will lessen the chance that your children will be a target of cyberbullies by offering features that:

- restrict your children's ability to give out personal information;
- block access to unmonitored chat rooms or inappropriate web sites;
- block the sending or receiving of e-mail with offensive information;
- send copies of your children's e-mail to your e-mail address;
- record the web sites they have visited as well as all messages they have sent and received.

As one example, you might consider using the Google Safe Search filtering tool that can be accessed by going to www.google.com/familysafety/tools.html.

Provide your children with the most important tool for preventing cyberbullying—good judgment.

Stress to them the importance of being respectful of others and not doing or saying anything they would not want done to themselves. You can help them exercise good decision-making by emphasizing how painful it is to be cyberbullied and the potential consequences of being caught harassing their peers.

Parent Strategies for Dealing with Cyberbullying

Be aware of signs that suggest your children are being cyberbullied. The more signs you see and the more atypical they are for your children, the greater the likelihood that there is a problem. These signs include:

- a reluctance to use the computer;
- secretiveness about online activities;
- anxiety upon receiving a computer or text message;
- withdrawn, sad behavior;
- changes in sleeping or eating habits;
- quickness to anger;
- avoidance of peers;
- resistance to going to school.

Take reports from your children of cyberbullying seriously. Respond in a sympathetic manner and do not blame them or get angry with them. If you respond in a helpful, supportive manner, they will be more likely to come to you next time there is a problem. Being harassed online can be a painful ordeal, and acknowledging this to their parents can be awkward and embarrassing.

Try to identify the cyberbully. Talk with your child and try to identify who is responsible for the harassment. The content or wording of the messages may suggest the identity. Ask if the online bullying is related to an issue with a student in school, and if so try to resolve that situation by contacting a school administrator and asking that he or she deal with the situation in school.

Help your child block the sender of these messages. The web site your child is on likely has a block feature that prevents those you designate from getting access to your computer.

Talk with your children about how to handle further incidents. You might tell them that if they receive additional messages, they should not respond to them and instead log off and then tell an adult. If they feel compelled to answer, tell them to take a break before responding so they are less likely to answer in an angry or provocative manner. See page 43 of this chapter entitled Technology Do's and Don't's for Children and Teens for more tips on how to deal with cyberbullying.

Google your child. This will help you determine if the cyberbully is posting offensive comments about your child online. You might conduct various searches, entering your child's full name, nickname and screen name as well as his or her cell number and address. For further information on how to do this, go to www.stopcyberbullying.org/take_action/google_yourself.html. The Google web site also has a feature that will alert you whenever information about your child is posted online.

Consider reporting the cyberbully to the Internet Service Provider (ISP) or the cell phone company. If someone is sending your child offensive text messages by cell phone, try tracing the number and reporting it to your phone service provider; you might also request a new number for your child. If someone is sending your child offensive messages via the computer, consider informing the sender's Internet Service Provider which has the power to terminate the account. You should contact your own ISP if your child's account has been hacked, his/her password compromised or if someone is posing as your child. If the cyberbullying is occurring on a social networking site, contact the web site by using the reporting feature. Companies and organizations take these reports seriously and can be helpful in curtailing the inappropriate behavior. Keep records of the messages your child receives so that you have a paper trail.

Consider reporting the cyberbully to the police. If the cyberbullying reaches the level you consider to be a serious threat, you should contact the police. At the same time your child needs to end any online communications with this person. You may also want to notify law enforcement if someone is posting your child's offline contact information on the Internet or is orchestrating a cyberbullying campaign that is being joined by others. If you contact the police, make sure to preserve as much electronic evidence as you can by not erasing any comments or pictures from the computer.

Take action if you find that your children are engaged in cyberbullying. Parents may suspect that their children are engaged in cyberbullying if they are especially preoccupied with online activity and extremely secretive about their online communications (for example, they minimize the screen when you walk past). If you discover that they have been sending offensive messages to others or engaging in other cyberbullying behaviors, talk with them and help them understand how hurtful these comments can be to others. At the same time state in no uncertain terms that this behavior is unacceptable and must stop immediately. If it continues, consider barring them from going online for a set period of time. You will also want to monitor closely their future online activity. In addition, you might install filtering software on the computer, which will limit their ability to send e-mails with offensive information. As a general rule of thumb, do not allow your children to engage in behaviors online that you would not tolerate in your home if your child was interacting with a peer.

Encourage your children to take action if they witness someone else being cyberbullied. The reality is that children are more likely to become aware of cyberbullying than adults. Let your children know that they are not to participate in any way in cyberbullying even if it was initiated by someone else. In addition, encourage them to try to stop cyberbullying incidents they encounter or else report them to an adult.

The School's Role

While most incidents of cyberbullying are initiated at home, schools are nonetheless feeling the effects of this high-tech form of harassment. Often they have to deal with student distress, anger and conflict that may accompany cyberbullying incidents that originate out of school. In addition, schools are facing an increasing number of cyberbullying problems that are initiated in school, either on school computers or students' cell phones. Whether the cyberbullying originates in school or at home, it is a problem that schools cannot afford to ignore.

Schools face a difficult dilemma in dealing with cyberbullying. While schools typically have limited authority over student actions conducted off school grounds, they do have a responsibility to ensure a safe and secure school climate and minimize disruptions to the educational process. The question is what is their authority and responsibility in dealing with cyberbullying incidents that are initiated on computers or cell phones outside of school but that give rise to student distress or disruptions in school.

Schools may be fearful of being sued for disciplining students for off-campus acts, but they are not powerless in dealing with these situations. Schools may exercise authority over off-campus acts if those acts disrupt the educational process in a clearly demonstrable way or significantly effect one or more students' well-being. This might include a physical or verbal altercation between students, a resulting severe decline in a student's school performance, emotional distress of a student, or a significant disruption of school activities. In sum, there must be some specific impact, or potential impact, on students or the educational process for the school to have authority to deal with both the problem and its cyberbullying origins. This standard of requiring a significant school impact to justify school intervention is consistent with Federal court rulings.

School Strategies for Preventing Cyberbullying

Develop a school cyberbullying policy. The school bullying policy should be expanded to include cyberbullying. This policy should define cyberbullying, describe the rules of acceptable use of technology in the schools, state the range of disciplinary consequences for violating these rules, and describe what students should do if they have been victimized by cyberbullying. The policy might also include a statement that the school district may intervene with cyberbullying incidents that originate out of school if they cause a significant disruption of the educational environment or substantially affect student well-being. Given the complex constitutional issues of disciplining students for off-school behavior, this policy should be developed in consultation with an attorney well-versed in school law.

Schools should consider sending these policies home in the beginning of the year and requiring signatures from both students and parents indicating that they have reviewed them. Informing parents of the school's policy will strengthen its ability to respond effectively to cyberbullying incidents. This policy might also be posted on the school's web site. Schools are now being advised to consider a special policy to address behaviors in social networks.

Include cyberbullying in the school's code of conduct. The code of conduct should define what cyberbullying is and what the range of consequences are for this behavior. The content should be consistent with the school cyberbullying policy. The code should be reviewed periodically and revised in accordance with new developments in technology.

Survey students and school staff about cyberbullying. School officials can obtain useful information about the nature and frequency of cyberbullying in their school by going to the primary source, namely students. Towards this end, schools might administer a written survey of students or conduct student focus groups. A survey appropriate for students can be found in Nancy Willard's book entitled, Cyberbullying and Cyberthreats: Responding to the Challenge of Online Social Aggression, Threats, and Distress (Research Press, 2007). If you conduct a survey, make sure that parents are informed of this survey and have the right to decline participation by their child. The school might also consider surveying school staff, especially administrators, guidance counselors, computer teachers and school resource officers.

Educate staff about cyberbullying. Schools should consider providing workshops to staff who may confront this problem, including administrators, teachers, guidance counselors, school librarians, paraprofessionals, school resource officers and computer lab coordinators. These forums should include the following topics:

- Basic facts about cyberbullying;
- Forms of cyberbullying;
- Prevalence and impact of cyberbullying;
- Ways to detect cyberbullying;
- The school district's cyberbullying policy and code of conduct;
- Strategies for preventing cyberbullying;
- Strategies for dealing with cyberbullying incidents.

Discuss cyberbullying with students. Schools need to talk with students about appropriate and inappropriate use of technology, perhaps in their computer classes or in an assembly. The following are some key points that need to be made to students:

- Delineate the rules regarding the use of the Internet, computers and cell phones while in school.
- Discuss the proper and ethical use of the Internet. (See page 43 at the end of this chapter, section entitled Technology Do's and Don't's for Children and Teens for a list of tips that need to be reinforced with students.)
- Talk with students about the pain of being cyberbullied, including how hurtful offensive messages can be, and elicit their thoughts and experiences.
- Advise students to seek help from an adult if they are being victimized by cyberbullying.
- Encourage students to respond in a helpful way if they witness cyberbullying by trying to stop the incident, support the victim or inform an adult. Be

emphatic in stating that they are not to encourage or support the cyberbully in any way.

- Explain the school's disciplinary approach to cyberbullying, which might be described in the following way. Any incident of peer harassment in school through either the computer or cell phone will be treated as a serious disciplinary matter. Students should also understand that they may be subject to discipline in school for inappropriate online behavior initiated outside of school if such behavior disrupts school activities or causes another student emotional distress.

- Discuss with students how their Internet and cell phone communications leave "digital footprints" that may allow them to be identified and thus held accountable for inappropriate actions. Internet Service Providers may identify the names of individuals who are engaging in improper online behavior in response to requests from law enforcement officials.

- Explain to students that some Internet activities, such as hacking, password theft, and identify theft, may be considered criminal acts that are punishable by law. If done on school grounds, these behaviors may give rise to serious disciplinary measures.

Present a formal cyberbullying curriculum to students. Various curricula have been developed for students at various grade levels. This program might be incorporated into the school's health education or technology programs or made part of a more comprehensive anti-bullying program. It might also be offered by a counselor in a small- or large-group format. It is intended to raise student awareness of cyberbullying and its impact on others, provide students with the skills to use technology in a safe, respect-ful and responsible manner, and teach them how to deal with cyberbullying incidents. It might also be incorporated into a program on social-emotional learning.

An important part of cyberbullying education is to teach students how to engage in social problem-solving and conflict resolution. This includes helping students learn what they should do if they observe other students being cyber-bullied. We know from research with face-to-face bullying that it can be stopped effectively by observers who are will-ing to take action. Similarly cyberbullying can be stopped in the same way. This program might include presentation of different scenarios, role-playing and group discussion.

An intended outcome is that students come to see cyberbullying as cruel and hurtful and hear others express the idea that they don't want to be friends with someone who would act that way towards others. If successful, cyberbullying education will make students less likely to send a nasty e-mail, less likely to spread a malicious rumor about a classmate, less likely to vote in negative polls about class-mates, and more likely to intervene when they see a cyber-bullying incident taking place.

Use peer mentoring. Consider having older stu-dents talk with younger students about appropriate and inappropriate ways of using the Internet. Peer mentors will have both credibility and influence with younger students on these issues.

Post information in school about cyberbullying. Signs or posters might be placed in the computer rooms, the library, hallways, classrooms and the guidance office. In addition, schools might place a list of its rules for technology use next to school computers as well as on the school web site.

Bring in a law enforcement official to talk with middle- or high-school students. This presentation might help students appreciate the potential seriousness of cyberbullying. The presenter might, for example, inform them that their Internet communications are not as anonymous as they might think by explaining that Internet Service Providers have the technology to identify the writer of IMs and e-mails. In addition, he/she might discuss, and perhaps even demonstrate, how each time a person uses the Internet it leaves an electronic "fingerprint" that can be used to trace these communications.

Make use of the school resource officer. School-based police officers may be knowledgeable about the legal aspects of cyberbullying. Even if a cyberbullying incident does not appear to raise legal concerns, the officer can still be helpful by meeting with students who engaged in cyberbullying and talking with their parents. His involvement will convey to the students and parents the potential seriousness of cyberbullying. The officer might also make presentations to classes about cyberbullying and emphasize to students the ways in which cyberbullying might give rise to potential legal problems.

Make parents aware of the perils of cyberbullying. Schools must also educate parents about this high-tech form of bullying, focusing on what they can do to help their children use the Internet in a safe and responsible manner. This may take the form of sending an informational handout to parents or holding a workshop for them to discuss these concerns. Content for such meetings with parents can be found in the earlier part of this chapter.

School Strategies for Dealing with Cyberbullying

Establish and communicate clear rules to staff for handling cyberbullying. Make sure all school staff are aware of who they should report cyberbullying incidents to and how they should handle inappropriate use of cell phones.

Provide students with an anonymous or confidential way of reporting cyberbullying. The school might place a box in the guidance office or main office for this purpose. If students do not trust that the source of the information will be kept confidential, they will be much less likely to report cyberbullying incidents to school personnel.

Respond to cyberbullying incidents quickly. It is important that schools send a message to students that they take reports of cyberbullying seriously by investigating promptly when incidents are brought to their attention and taking action when appropriate.

Tailor discipline to the severity of the incident. It is not enough just to have cyberbullying incorporated into the code of conduct. School officials must also respond to reports of cyberbullying and take appropriate action. While suspension may be warranted in response to severe cyberbullying incidents, it can sometimes be counterproductive if it causes the punished student to spend time at home seeking revenge by continuing to harass the victim in perhaps more anonymous ways. Schools should be creative in finding disciplinary methods for minor cyberbullying incidents (for example, having the student write a paper on how cyberbullying can affect children or having the student speak to students in a lower grade about cyberbullying).

The school also needs to use counseling and mediation methods to deal with these incidents. Counseling can help the student understand the impact of the cyberbullying on the victim and experience remorse or regret for the harassment so that he/she is less likely to repeat this behavior. Also the student should be helped to understand the impact of the cyberbullying on his/her reputation with classmates. If the cyberbullying relates to a conflict with the victim, try to resolve this disagreement. You will also want to notify the parents of both the offending party and the victim, and perhaps bring them in for a conference.

Keep a record of computer activity. Schools might consider installing software that can maintain a record of all online activity conducted on school computers. If a school opts to do this, it must disclose this information in its technology policy. Students' awareness of the school's capacity to keep track of this information will likely deter them from sending inappropriate messages on school computers.

Provide support to the victim. As noted above, victims of cyberbullying can experience emotional distress and even trauma. Provide counseling support to this student upon learning of the incident and continue to monitor his/her emotional well-being in school.

Technology Do's and Don't's for Children and Teens

Tips for Preventing Cyberbullying

- Do not give information to people you meet online that allows them to contact you; this includes your name, instant message name, screen name, school name, e-mail address, street address or cell phone number. Similarly do not post information online (for example, on a social networking profile or an away message) that can be hurtful to you if sent to others.

- Do not say or post anything in a chat room, on a bulletin board or on a social networking site that you would not want made public.

- Do not give out your password. In addition, make sure to uncheck the "remember password" setting when on a computer in a public or school library, or even at a friend's home.

- Use a screen name different from your e-mail address when you are in a chat room or sending an instant message. Make sure your screen name does not convey personal information. Also do not exchange e-mails with someone you have met in a chat room.

- Recognize that people online are not always who they say they are. People often pretend to be others for a wide variety of reasons.

- Do not attack or provoke anyone online. In the language of cyberspace, you do not want to engage in "flaming." Doing this not only risks your becoming embroiled in an online confrontation with others but it may also violate the "terms of service" of your Internet Service Provider and result in sanctions.

- Review what you write before sending an online message so as to avoid saying something that may be perceived as offensive.

- Do not use all capital letters when posting. This is equivalent to yelling online and may provoke others.

- Never make threats online. Even if made in anger or in jest, the recipient may report this threat and you may find yourself in trouble at school or with the law.

- Avoid making controversial statements related to sensitive topics (for example, race, religion or gender issues) if you do not know the people you are communicating with online. These statements can easily trigger cyberbullying incidents. Be especially respectful when speaking online with people from other cultures or countries. What you may assume to be acceptable statements or beliefs can be offensive to people from different backgrounds.

• Resolve online misunderstandings quickly. If others take offense at something you have posted, don't hesitate to apologize. You might ask them what it was that was objectionable and, if appropriate, let them know they misunderstood what you said.

• Employ sharing controls and privacy settings. Many sites where users provide information such as You Tube and social networking sites such as Facebook have sharing controls that enable users to decide who is allowed to see personal blogs, profiles, pictures and images. The more personal the information shared on these sites, the more important it is to restrict who is allowed access. Similarly, most Instant Messaging programs have a feature that allows users to block individuals they don't want to contact them.

• Do not allow individuals you suspect of cyberbullying to include you on their buddy list. This feature is often found in the privacy setting or parent control section of the web site. Cyberbullies can use the buddy list as a way of keeping track of when people they are targeting are online.

• Never arrange to meet someone in person you have met online unless your parents are present. Remember that people are not always who they say they are.

- Do not identify people by name in public profiles or pictures. In this way you are protecting their privacy.

Tips for Dealing with Cyberbullying Incidents

- Consider not responding to a provocative or offensive e-mail, especially if it is more in the nature of a prank or mild teasing. The sender is often looking for a reaction and he/she is likely to simply stop if there is no response. It isn't easy to ignore a hurtful comment directed at you, but a response in kind risks your becoming caught up in an online confrontation that can quickly spin out of control.

- If you are angry and determined to counter an offensive post, take a break to cool down before you respond. If you answer while in the throes of anger, you run the risk of falling into the trap of becoming a cyberbully yourself. Make sure to review what you have written before you press the send button, avoiding language that inflames the situation. Once you have sent a response, it is too late to take it back. A non-confrontational response might be to simply say "stop" to the sender of the original message.

- If the person continues to send you upsetting messages despite your requests that he/she stop, terminate the online relationship. This might mean leaving a chat room or blocking the person from communicating with you. By accessing the blocking feature provided by most Internet Service Providers, the cyberbully will not know when you are online or be able to contact you through the web site.

- Consider changing your e-mail address if someone persists in sending you harassing e-mails.

- If your efforts to terminate the online relationship are unsuccessful and the person continues to harass you, talk with an adult who may have other ways of dealing with the cyberbullying. These other options include contacting the Internet Service Provider (or cell phone provider if it the messages are sent by text) as well as law enforcement officials. If you do pursue one of these options, it will be important for you to save the offensive messages that have been sent to you, noting the date and time of the messages.

- If you have received threats online, contact an adult immediately. These threats may warrant your parents contacting the police.

Chapter 3
A Comprehensive Program to Prevent Bullying

As discussed in the first chapter, bullying is a pervasive school problem that can have serious consequences for students. Fortunately it is a problem that schools can do something about. Research indicates that when schools implement a comprehensive program of bullying prevention, they can significantly reduce this problem. In fact, studies by Professor Dan Olweus, a Norwegian psychologist who is considered the world's foremost authority on bullying, show that bullying incidents can be cut in half by implementing a school-wide anti-bullying program. These two factors—the seriousness of the bullying problem and the demonstrated potential for schools to significantly curtail this problem—compel all schools to consider implementing a program to prevent bullying. This chapter offers such a program, namely a twelve-step bullying prevention program that schools can implement at the elementary and middle school level.

Bullying Prevention: A Comprehensive Approach

For a bullying prevention program to be effective, it must be comprehensive in the true sense of the word. It must include specific strategies designed to effect change at three levels: the school, the classroom, and the individual students. It must also embrace the entire school community. All adult members of the school community, including parents, administrators, teachers, counselors, psychologists, nurses, coaches, paraprofessionals, secretaries, bus drivers, custodians and after-school staff, should participate in the program inasmuch as they are all in a position to witness acts of bullying and take steps to intervene if they do.

The program must also target for behavioral and attitudinal change the entire student population, even those in kindergarten and first grade. Bullying can happen at any grade level. The program should not be limited to those who are prone to bullying or at risk for being bullied. Other students—the bystanders—can play a key role in preventing bullying by learning how to respond when they witness incidents; thus they need to be part of the program.

A bullying prevention program must of course deal with individual students, but it must also address the school culture. This means taking steps to ensure that staff and students come to see the prevention of bullying as a core value and belief of the school. To achieve this result, bullying prevention cannot be limited to a single assembly or a one-time lecture by the teacher. Rather the values that underlie bullying prevention—empathy, caring, respect, and responsibility—must be articulated on a continuing basis, in a diversity of ways, and by a variety of individuals.

Towards this end, it is important to promote a climate of cooperation and caring by reinforcing acts of kindness and communicating the above values. The most effective way to foster a caring attitude in school is for all staff to model this behavior by listening attentively to students and taking their concerns seriously, by speaking with them in a warm, respectful manner, by acknowledging their successes, and by providing them encouragement.

Steps of the Bullying Prevention Program

This section describes a 12-step bullying prevention program that was designed with the above considerations in mind. It is comprehensive in nature in that:

- it offers interventions at the school level, the classroom level and the individual student level
- it recognizes the importance of participation by the entire school community
- it involves the entire student population, including those who are doing the bullying, those who are being bullied and those who are bystanders
- it addresses the school culture, examining ways that the school can promote values that discourage bullying behavior

Each of the following 12 components plays a key role in combating bullying. While schools will likely help to reduce bullying by implementing some of the components, they will only achieve the full preventative effect if they implement all of the components that make up this bullying prevention program.

1. Establish a committee to develop a school bullying policy and coordinate bullying prevention activities.

This might be an already existing group such as the school safety committee or it might be a committee established for just this purpose. This committee should receive training in bullying prevention and meet regularly during the year. It should be led by the principal and include at a minimum a teacher, a pupil services professional, a paraprofessional, a bus driver and a parent. It might also include a student who is believed capable of contributing the student perspective and who can give insight into how students will react to aspects of the program. Choose committee members who can communicate effectively and are committed to the concept of working as a team. An important part of the committee's mission will be to convince school staff of the importance of this topic and to justify the time and effort they will need to put into implementing the program.

In developing policies and procedures for handling bullying, the committee might want to discuss the following questions:

- How is bullying to be defined? What are some examples?
- What are the consequences for bullying?
- Under what circumstances will parents be informed of a bullying incident?
- What steps will be taken to provide guidance to the bully and victim?
- How do students report bullying? To whom? Will there be a bullying box?
- What should staff do if they witness a bullying incident or are informed of an incident by a student?
- What are the procedures for keeping track of bullying incidents?

- What is the relationship of a bullying policy to other polices of student conduct?
- How will the school evaluate the effectiveness of the bullying prevention program?
- How will staff, parents and students be informed of the school policies on bullying?

2. Conduct a survey of students about bullying.

An important part of a bullying prevention program is understanding the dimensions of the problem in the school. An effective way of obtaining this information is to conduct an anonymous survey of students. In the survey there should be questions that will elicit the following information:

- prevalence of bullying
- types of bullying behavior that are taking place
- areas where bullying incidents are occurring; these are often related to as the school "hot spots" (the survey might include a map of the school and ask students to mark where bullying is most likely to occur)
- activities where bullying incidents are occurring
- attitudes of students about bullying
- steps taken by students to deal with bullying and the results
- suggestions about what the school can do to deal with bullying

This survey might be given to all students in the school who have the ability to complete the form. This might mean rewording it to reflect the needs of various grade levels. It is also acceptable to use an already developed survey such as can be found in *The Bullying Prevention Handbook* by John H. Hoover and Ronald Oliver (see Chapter 9 for complete citation). These surveys can be reproduced for use by schools.

The bullying prevention committee will want to use the results of this survey in designing the program. The data will help staff understand the magnitude of the bullying problem by pinpointing how often it is happening, where it is occurring and what forms it is taking. These results will be helpful to school staff in identifying behaviors that they need to be targeting and in suggesting areas of the school that need more supervision.

A survey of bullying behavior can also be used to evaluate the effectiveness of the program. Indeed, the evaluation of the program's effectiveness is an essential part of any effort to curtail bullying. Towards this end, it is important to do a pre-and post-survey, namely administer it before the program is implemented and then after it has been in effect for a substantial period. These results can then be charted and analyzed to assess the impact of the program. The results of this evaluation can also be used to fine-tune the program. The survey can also be given to students on a regular basis (perhaps once or twice a year) to monitor the status of bullying in the school.

Of course, efforts to evaluate the effectiveness of a bullying prevention program should not be limited to the results of a survey. Schools may also examine data related to disciplinary measures (for example, the number of suspensions and detentions) as well as consider anecdotal observations of staff regarding peer interactions. Schools that have effective bullying prevention programs may observe a decrease in other anti-social behavior such as fighting, vandalism and theft.

Schools might also survey teachers and parents to elicit their observations about school bullying. In addition to including questions to reflect the student survey categories, there might also be questions which will probe the adults' views of the school's bullying procedures and policies, as well as their ideas for dealing with bullying.

3. Establish a clear policy prohibiting bullying and then communicate it to students, staff and parents.

This policy might be incorporated into an existing written code of conduct or may be a stand-alone document. It should include at minimum a definition of bullying, a clear statement that bullying of any kind is prohibited, a description of the possible consequences for bullying, and instructions for students who witness bullying. It is not sufficient to have a policy that just prohibits physical aggression. It must be specific to all forms of bullying.

The policy should be reviewed with staff so they are clear about what is expected of them if they observe or are told of a bullying incident. It should also be communicated to students in such a way that it is hard for them to ignore. It might be decided, for example, to hold an assembly every year to discuss the policy. In addition, parents need to be informed of the policy, perhaps through a special letter home or through the school newsletter. Parents might be asked to discuss and reinforce the policy with their children; it might also be requested that they and their children sign the document and return it.

4. Provide close and adequate supervision of areas where, and times when, bullying is likely to occur.

Bullying often takes place outside of the classroom.

The following are areas/times where bullying is common:
- hallways
- bus
- bus stop
- playground
- locker room
- cafeteria
- bathroom
- extracurricular events
- walking to and from school

While paraprofessionals play a key monitoring role during these less structured activities, the principal or assistant principal also needs to supervise these areas on a regular or periodic basis. An administrator might meet with paraprofessionals on occasion to review issues of concern and discuss particular students. If additional supervision is needed, consider using parent volunteers if paid assistance is unavailable. Guidance counselors and school psychologists might also be used during lunch and recess to observe and deal with incidents of bullying.

5. Provide training for teachers and other school staff on bullying.

Because teachers and paraprofessionals are with students most of the day, they play key roles in observing and dealing with incidents of bullying. To do this job most effectively, they need training in learning how to prevent bullying, recognizing the signs of bullying, and knowing what to do when incidents occur. This training might also discuss how teachers can integrate bullying themes into their classroom lessons, perhaps in concert with character education programs and social emotional learning activities.

Other school staff members should be trained as well. An effective bullying prevention program requires that the principal enlist the entire school in the campaign. All staff members, including faculty, paraprofessionals, bus drivers, coaches, after-school supervisors, secretaries, and custodians, should be provided with information about the bullying prevention program and their specific roles and responsibilities regarding bullying.

6. Raise student and staff awareness about bullying through school-wide activities.

An essential component of a bullying prevention program is raising students' awareness about the problem of bullying through school activities. These activities help to remind students about the school policy regarding bullying and the importance of supporting their classmates. In addition, they help to generate energy for the program. While these awareness-raising activities are not sufficient by themselves to confront the problem of bullying, they can make an immediate impact in reducing bullying incidents. There are presently some excellent videos available for this very purpose. If time allows, consideration might be given to having a day with a full range of activities devoted to the anti-bullying campaign. Here are some specific activities that could be considered:

School Assembly — Students need to have the bullying policy explained to them in school. This is best done at a school-wide assembly that is focused exclusively on the issue of bullying. At this assembly the principal or other staff members might aim to do the following:

- explain the bullying policy
- define what bullying is and give some examples
- discuss the consequences of bullying
- help students understand what it feels like to be bullied
- make it clear to students that they are not to join in when they observe a child being bullied
- discuss the role of bystander
- explain what steps they can take if they observe a classmate being bullied, namely informing an adult and if comfortable supporting the victim
- include discussion of cyberbullying

Schools might use methods other than lecture to convey this information. They might arrange for an outside speaker to talk to students or for older students to present a skit. They might also show a video about bullying intended for students (see Chapter 9 for a list of these videos).

Posters — A common way of raising students' awareness of bullying is to have students create anti-bullying posters or signs that are displayed throughout the school. These might be created in the regular classroom or in art class, or commercial ones can be purchased.

Brochure — The distribution of a brochure describing in terms that can be understood what the bullying policy is and what students should do if they are bullied or they see another student being bullied. They might be encouraged to staple this inside their notebooks.

Buttons — There can be a contest asking students to come up with an anti-bullying slogan to be put on buttons to be worn by students. Companies are available that will make buttons.

Anti-Bullying Pledge — Students might be asked to take a pledge such as the one that follows. It is a call to action if bullying is witnessed.

> This is for me, my friends today, and my friends tomorrow. I think being mean stinks. I won't watch someone get picked on. Because I am a do something person, not a do nothing person, I care. I can help change things. I can be a leader. In my world there are no bullies allowed. Bullying is bad. Bullying bites. Bullying bothers me. I know sticking up for someone is the right thing to do. My name is (your name). And I won't stand by. I will stand up. (From www.bullying.org)

Rumor Pledge — Students may be asked to sign a pledge not to say or do hurtful things to classmates. An example of a simply stated pledge is as follows: "I solemnly promise not to spread a rumor about another person in my school or community for the rest of the school year."

Mix-Up Day — Some school districts have what they call "mix-up days" in which students sit at other than their usual lunchtime tables. Additionally teachers may want to group students who would not ordinarily interact with each other, during cooperative learning groups, on field trips, etc.

Recognition of Appropriate Behavior — Just as there should be an effort to discourage bullying behavior through school and classroom activities, there should be a similar effort to encourage behaviors that are inconsistent with bullying. The following are some ways that teachers can promote kind behavior in their classrooms:

- Teachers might put up a courtesy display on their bulletin board where they would post acts of kindness they observe by their students. They might also encourage their students to tell them about courteous acts of classmates for posting on the display.

- Teachers might have a raffle in which they give tickets to students who have engaged in acts of kindness. The students then deposit the tickets in a box after writing their name on them. At the end of the week the teacher draws a ticket from the box and rewards the student with the winning ticket with a prize or privilege.

- Teachers might reward their entire class for acts of kindness by their students. One way of doing this is for teachers to deposit a marble in a jar on their desk every time they observe an act of kindness by a student. Once the jar is full, the teacher can give the class a special prize or privilege.

- Teachers might encourage kind behavior by giving a student who has acted in a courteous manner a "kindness necklace" to wear. The student is then encouraged to pass the necklace on to another student who has acted kindly. While teachers might only use this strategy on a periodic basis, they should let their students know that they expect them to act kindly all year round.

7. Integrate bullying lessons and activities into the classroom curriculum.

Teachers have various opportunities to weave bullying themes into their curriculum. This might take the form of conducting a lesson about bullying, having students read a book about bullying followed by a classroom discussion, or having a classroom meeting focused exclusively on the issue of bullying. These strategies are discussed in greater detail in Chapter 5.

8. Empower bystanders to support the victims of bullying.

While school staff are often unaware that bullying is taking place, other students are typically not only aware of the incidents but present when they occur. These bystanders to bullying can thus play a crucial role in helping to address the problem. According to Dr. Debra Pepler of York University in Canada, bullying stopped in less than 10 seconds a majority of the time that a classmate intervened. In short, the goal is to try to turn the silent majority of students into a caring majority. Bystanders will help if they know what to do.

Students can assist classmates who are being bullied by telling the bully to stop or by reaching out to the victim in friendship or support. But the most important thing they can do is to report any bullying incidents to a school staff member. Keep in mind that students may be reluctant to do this because they do not want to be seen as a tattletale so they need to understand that telling about bullying is very different from tattling on a student. The point might be made that telling is what you do to get someone out of trouble and tattling is what you do to get someone in trouble. In this way the school can become a "telling school".

It is more likely that students will report bullying when their names are kept anonymous and when they are reinforced for reporting incidents. Students will more likely come forward if they are confident the bully will not know who did the reporting and if they see staff responding seriously to their reports and taking action. One way of encouraging student reports is to set up a box in the school, perhaps in the guidance counselor's or nurse's office, where students can deposit notes about bullying incidents they have either experienced or witnessed. Students should be encouraged to sign the note and identify the bully by name while assuring their anonymity. This box should be locked, with the contents available only to designated school staff. Rather than identifying this as a bullying box, students might be told that it is for anyone to use if they have a concern to which they want to bring attention. In this way, students using this box will not be identified as necessarily reporting about bullying.

9. Involve parents/guardians in the program.

Parents are valuable members of the bullying prevention team. They can provide assistance in various ways. First, they can be an important source of information about bullying incidents, but if they do come forward it is critical that schools take their concerns seriously and respond forcefully. Second, parents need to be informed of school policies regarding bullying and encouraged to reinforce this policy with their children. This includes parents who are enrolling their child during the course of the year. Third, parents may be surveyed to elicit their views and knowledge of bullying in the school. Fourth, parents need to be informed if their child has been bullied or has been bullying another child. The purpose of informing them is not to criticize them but rather to help them support their child. They may need assistance with steps to take at home, so a face-to-face meeting is usually best. At this meeting they should be provided with a plan of action on how the bullying will be handled in school, and asked for their support. If their child was the one doing the bullying, it is important to avoid suggestions that they are blameworthy even if it is concluded that they may have contributed to their child's bullying behavior with inappropriate messages. The discussion needs to be solution-focused. More information about involving the parents is to be found in Chapter 6. It is also recommended that consideration be given to utilizing the specific parent tape of this series, as it provides both the background as well as specifics for them to use with their children. It will enable them to become more equal partners in the effort to prevent and control bullying.

10. Pay special attention to students who are at risk for being bullied.

Students are more likely to be bullied if they:

- are isolated from their classmates
- are in special education programs
- speak English as a second language
- have some physical characteristic that makes them stand out from their peers (for example, they are short, overweight, stutter or have an accent)
- are new to the school

Students who are loners are especially vulnerable. Put another way, students are less likely to be bullied if they are around other children during much of the school day. The chance of these students being bullied is lessened when they are provided with appropriate support. For example, students who are new to the school or who tend to be isolated should be helped to become more involved with their peers by integrating them into classroom and playground activities, by pairing them with students who are likely to be accepting, and by making sure they do not eat lunch alone.

11. Take reports of bullying seriously and act quickly.

As discussed in the first chapter, school staff do not always respond with the appropriate level of concern upon learning of bullying incidents. It is important to remedy this problem by encouraging them to respond to all reports of bullying that come to their attention. An incident may appear minor to them but may loom large to the student.

The principal must communicate to school staff in a clear and direct manner the importance of attending to all reports of bullying. While teachers and other staff may not always be able to give immediate attention to bullying incidents, they need to make sure that they respond to the incident in some way before the end of the day, or bring it to the attention of another staff member such as the principal or guidance counselor. The faster staff are able to respond to bullying incidents, the more they can lessen the pain to the victim and the greater the impact in curtailing bullying.

Responding to all reports of bullying will not only send a strong message to bullies that they will be held accountable for their behavior but will also send a strong message to other students that staff will protect them. If students sense this, they will be more likely to seek the assistance of staff because they will be more confident their concerns will be taken seriously.

While school staff may not always observe or be informed about a bullying incident, they may see behaviors from a child that indicate that he or she may be a victim. Chapter 1 describes various warning signs that may suggest that a child has been bullied. School staff need to be encouraged to be alert for these signs and follow up by talking with the student.

12. Respond to bullying incidents with a combination of disciplinary and guidance strategies.

Despite your best efforts to prevent bullying, incidents will no doubt happen. When they do, it is essential that school staff work with both students, providing the bully with appropriate discipline as well as guidance, and providing the victim with emotional support as well as help in developing coping skills to deal with future incidents. There needs to be a mechanism in place for providing counseling help to both bullies and victims. If counseling is not available in school, staff need to provide referrals to local mental health agencies.

Chapter 4
The Roles of the Administrator and Pupil Services Staff

Any effort to prevent bullying must begin with the school's administration. As with any school practice, the principal must provide leadership and vision as well as set the tone. In the case of bullying, a strong message must be sent by the principal that keeping students safe is an essential part of the school's mission. It must be made crystal clear that bullying will not be tolerated. But, as we have seen in the previous chapter, preventing bullying requires more than just sending a strong message. It also demands a coordinated school-wide campaign in which all members of the school community, including school staff, students and parents, work together to reduce and ultimately eliminate bullying.

In this chapter we will take a look at some specific steps administrators and pupil services staff, namely guidance counselors, psychologists, social workers and nurses, can take to respond to the bully and the victim in a way that makes bullying less likely in the future and provides support and guidance to the victim.

Dealing with the Bully

In responding to the bully, keep in mind that your first and foremost goal is to protect the victim by stopping the bullying behavior. You may conclude that you need to apply disciplinary measures to the student who did the bullying in an effort to deter future incidents. These consequences are most effective when they are certain, predictable and escalating.

In deciding upon disciplinary consequences, consider the nature of the bullying, the age of the student and his history of misbehavior. They might include:

- a conference with the principal
- parent contact
- restitution, namely return of items taken from the victim
- exclusion from the place or activity where the bullying occurred
- detention
- an assignment related to bullying (for example, writing an essay about what it might feel like to be bullied)
- withdrawal of school privileges
- community service
- behavior modification plan/contract
- suspension

A commonly used form of discipline is to temporarily exclude the student from the place or activity where the bullying took place. For example, if his bullying occurred during recess, he might be barred from the playground for a defined period. If he has been repeatedly taunting students on the school bus, he might lose the privilege of riding the bus for a set number of days. If he has been shoving and badgering other students in the hallway, he might be escorted from class to class by a school aide. If he has been ridiculing students next to him in class, his desk might be moved next to the teacher's desk.

Some contend that the best way to deal with a bully is to give him a dose of his own medicine. But you don't want to bully the bully by using harsh disciplinary measures. Acting in a way that humiliates or embarrasses the student may only fuel his anger and give rise to a desire for reprisal. Any disciplinary measures should be applied in a firm, but not a hostile manner.

Rather than thinking of discipline as a punishment, think of it as a teaching opportunity. Indeed, the word discipline is derived from the Latin word "disciplina," meaning instruction. In an effort to teach the bully how to behave appropriately, you need to convey the following to the student when disciplining him:

- describe the student's behavior and label it as bullying
- state the school rule that prohibits bullying
- indicate that he violated this rule and that he must stop this behavior immediately
- inform the student of the disciplinary consequences of his bullying behavior

Bullies often have little sympathy for their victims. One disciplinary measure that may help them understand the feelings of their victims is to assign them tasks that involve reaching out to others. Through specific community service activities, they may experience the rewards of helping others, which may prompt changes in the way they think about and relate to their peers. Examples of these tasks include:

- helping students with homework in an after-school program
- organizing a game for children in a lower grade during recess
- recording acts of kindness by students to help determine who receives school courtesy awards
- helping the principal monitor younger students in the lunchroom
- assisting a disabled student with an activity
- making a "No bullying" poster for display in the hallway

It is recommended that you contact the bully's parents with every bullying incident. The purpose is to inform them of what happened as well as encourage them to work with you to resolve the problem. In discussing the issue with them, be careful not to suggest that they are at fault or the cause of the problem even though you may have concerns about the messages they are giving their child. After discussing your course of action with them and hopefully eliciting their support, bring the student in and inform him of the plan. Make sure the student sees that you and the parents are in agreement. Try to get the parents to endorse the plan in their child's presence.

The bully needs to be disciplined to be sure but he also needs guidance, especially if this is a long-standing pattern. This means helping him understand why his behavior is unacceptable and find alternative behaviors. Providing the bully with guidance and counseling is especially important because bullies are prone to serious problems in the future, including an increased risk for dropping out of school, job-related problems, relationship difficulties and criminal activity.

Bullying behavior is a learned behavior, meaning that it can also be unlearned. Keep in mind that bullies bully for a reason, whether to gain status with their peers, to exert power over them, to punish another child, or to vent frustration with problems at home or in school. Your goal here is to identify the emotional needs that underlie the bullying and then provide the student with appropriate support such as helping him learn how to obtain attention or status from peers in more appropriate ways.

In an effort to help the bully, a guidance counselor or school psychologist might meet with the student in a counseling setting. He or she might try to connect with the bully by having a non-threatening discussion, listening attentively without condoning his behavior, and trying to find out what triggered his actions.

Many educators, both in regular and special education, are becoming familiar with the use of a Functional Behavioral Assessment (FBA). This activity provides more information about a behavior, most particularly the function or reason for the behavior, as well as the circumstances or triggers that precede it. By understanding factors related to a behavior, it is possible to address it and help the student develop an alternative behavior that will be acceptable. Certainly bullying is one of the behaviors for which an alternate, more socially acceptable behavior would be most welcome.

The counselor may also want to talk with the bully about his perceptions of the situation. Given that bullies are highly prone to misperceiving hostility where none is present, it is important to examine whether he has misperceived social cues and thus needs help with reading social situations correctly. This may involve considering what the bully thought the victim said or did, what he thought the victim was feeling, what were some other explanations for the victim's actions or comments, and finally some alternative ways the bully might have responded. In this way the bully can learn to rethink and reinterpret social situations. The counselor may also talk with the student about how his behavior will cause classmates to avoid him out of fear. If school counseling services are not available, the school might recommend the parents obtain mental health services for their child.

Role playing can be a useful strategy in working with the student, with the bully being asked to take on the roles of both bully and victim so that he can experience how it feels to be bullied and consider alternative responses to being aggressive.

Once you have provided the appropriate discipline and counseling support to the student, you need to monitor his behavior closely. If he continues to bully other students despite concerted efforts by school personnel to change his behavior and you conclude he represents a safety concern for students, consideration should be given to removing him from his class or even the school. The victim's program should not be changed to avoid coming into contact with the bully.

Dealing with the Victim

Just as the bully warrants your attention, so too does the victim. Unfortunately in many cases the bully gets more support from school staff than the child he bullied. Yet the victim often needs counseling help. Your success in counseling the victims of bullying will depend on your ability to establish trust with them in light of their likely embarrassment and reluctance to talk about what happened.

Ask what happened and listen sympathetically to his response. The victim needs a chance to tell the story of what happened to him. Acknowledge his distress and let him know you are sorry for what he experienced. Reassure him that he is not to blame for the bullying and praise him for his willingness to speak with you about it. Encourage the student to tell you or another school staff member of future bullying incidents as soon as possible and reassure him that the school will make every effort to stop them. Also make sure to inform his parents about the incident and let him know you are going to do this.

You may also want to help victims of bullying develop more effective coping skills although you want to make sure not to place responsibility on them for dealing with the bullying. In coaching the student how to respond, consider his age and the nature of the bullying. In some cases, you may want to teach him how to assert himself with the bully. If so, try role-playing with him, suggesting what he might say or do to deflect the taunting as well as project a greater air of confidence, but make sure he knows not to respond physically.

He does not need to respond with an elaborate or clever retort. Often the best response of a student who is being taunted is to make a brief comment such as "I don't like what you're saying so stop it" and then walk away. Bullies are often looking for targets who are likely to dissolve in tears or passively accept the harassment. A child who does not respond in a way that gives the bully what he wants is less likely to be targeted in the future. Chapter 7 gives some other examples of what the student might say.

In some cases you may conclude that the victim was engaging in provocative behavior. While you want to make sure that the bully understands that these behaviors do not justify his mistreatment of the student, nonetheless you may want to help the victim eliminate these actions from his behavioral repertoire. In doing this, consider what emotional need his behaviors were trying to satisfy (often peer status and acceptance) and then help him find more appropriate behaviors to meet those needs.

If the teacher does not already know about the bullying incident, let her know and also inform school staff involved with the student so they can monitor the situation. Also check with the student after a couple of days to find out if the bullying has stopped and then periodically after that. Even if the bullying has stopped, you may still want to provide him with guidance, particularly if he is isolated from his peers. For example, you may want to help him expand his friendships and develop his social skills.

In dealing with a bullying situation, one step you should rarely take is to treat the incident as a peer conflict and try to mediate a solution by getting the bully and victim together. If this is a true bullying situation, then there is an imbalance of power between the two students and probably no conflict to resolve. Getting them together is likely to be intimidating for the victim and may unfairly signal to him that he has done something wrong that needs to be resolved. Rather the message to the victim should be that the bully has acted inappropriately and school staff will take responsibility for resolving the problem. Conflict resolution procedures are more appropriate where there is parity between the students or fault on both sides.

Chapter 5
The Role of the Teacher

As a classroom teacher you are at the core of any bullying prevention program. You know your students better than any other staff member because you spend more time with them than anyone else in school. You know their strengths, their weaknesses and their vulnerabilities because you have the opportunity to observe them performing in a range of situations. You are thus well-positioned to observe bullying incidents with your students, to detect behavioral changes that may signal that a child has been bullied, to intervene when incidents occur, and to monitor the students to ensure that the bullying does not recur.

You also play a crucial role in preventing bullying. Prevention is at its essence a process of education, and many of the lessons that students need to learn that may dissuade them from engaging in bullying must come from you, whether through guidance to individual students or through instruction to your whole class by integrating anti-bullying lessons and positive social skill development into your curriculum.

When it comes to bullying, every one of your students, not just those who committed the bullying or were its victims, demands your attention. All students need assurance that you will respond seriously to bullying and take steps to protect them. Fortunately you have a variety of strategies available to you, for both preventing bullying and dealing with it when it does occurs. This chapter takes a close-up look at how you can accomplish those two goals.

Signs that a Student is Being Bullied

While teachers are the school adults who spend the most time with the students and thus know them best, it is unrealistic to expect that you will notice every bullying incident that takes place with your students. As previously discussed, bullying incidents often take place outside the classroom. In addition, victims of bullying often fail to report incidents to teachers because they are not confident teachers will take their concerns seriously or they fear retaliation. As a result, bullying is a problem that sometimes escapes detection by teachers. This makes it all the more important that teachers be on the lookout for behavioral signs suggesting that a child is being bullied, some of which are listed below. Of course, the more of these behaviors exhibited by a student, the more reason to suspect bullying.

- frequent school absences
- anxiety or fearfulness during class
- difficulty focusing in class
- unusual sadness
- withdrawal from peers
- a decline in academic performance
- not eating lunch
- avoidance of certain school areas
- clingy behavior

- frequent visits to the school nurse
- torn clothing or bruises

Ways to Bully-Proof Your Classroom

The most effective way to deal with bullying is to prevent it from happening in the first place. Dan Olweus, a Norwegian professor who is considered the "father" of bullying research, has designed a comprehensive program to prevent bullying that has been implemented in many American schools. His programs have led to a dramatic decline of as much as 50 percent in the rate of bullying, as discussed in his 1993 book, Bullying at School. Teachers play a vital role in his bullying prevention program and indeed in all such programs. The following are some specific teaching strategies you can use to bully-proof your classroom.

Foster a climate of cooperation and caring. You can help to prevent bullying by the tone you set in your classroom. More specifically, you can send an anti-bullying message by reinforcing acts of kindness and communicating values of tolerance, respect and responsibility. The most effective way to foster a caring attitude in your classroom is to model this behavior yourself by relating in a warm, sympathetic way with your students without talking down to them. As the saying goes, example is the best teacher.

Here are some specific strategies for promoting a cooperative and caring climate in your classroom:

- Avoid sarcasm or put-downs of any kind. If you are taking a child to task for misbehaving, you can talk to him in a firm manner and get your point across without being rude or impolite.
- Incorporate into your classroom lessons activities that promote understanding of those who are different.

77

- Consider using cooperative learning projects in which students must work together to attain success.

- Give out courtesy awards to younger students for such actions as helping a classmate with an assignment, comforting someone who is upset, inviting a new student to join in a game, or coming to the defense of a child who is being bullied.

- Establish a box that students can place notes in complimenting their classmates for something they said or did. At the end of the week read these notes to the class.

- Name a "student of the week" and then develop a poster about him that includes positive comments from classmates.

- Have a class meeting periodically in which students gather in a circle and compliment or express appreciation to a classmate. Only allow positive comments and make sure that all students are acknowledged at least every other meeting. You may need to get the ball rolling by being the first to talk about an act of kindness by a student.

- Have a courtesy display on the bulletin board. When you observe an act of kindness by one of your students, describe the act with the student's name on a 3 x 5 card or a heart-shaped piece of paper and tack it to the display. Encourage students to tell you about actions of classmates for posting on the display, or have them write out the cards and submit them to you. This may give rise to a chain reaction of compliments that has a contagious effect on your class.

Catch the bullying student being kind. Make a special effort to find something positive to say about students who are prone to unkind behavior, even if it is a small gesture. As an example, you might praise a student if you see him acting in a caring or helpful manner to a classmate. Describe the specific behavior that you observed as you praise him. Do this publicly (unless you think it would embarrass him) to encourage other children to engage in similar acts of kindness. As an example, you might say to a student: "Seth, it was so nice of you to sit with Julio after he hurt himself on the playground. That was a very caring thing to do."

Hold a classroom meeting early in the year to discuss bullying. This is an activity that all teachers can do with their classes, even with students as young as five or six. It may be difficult to find time to hold these meetings, especially at the middle-school level, but it is likely to be time well spent. Just discussing the problem of bullying with your class will raise their awareness of the issue and help to decrease bullying incidents. You may want to revisit the issue of bullying at periodic class meetings throughout the year.

You might want to begin the meeting by showing your class a video (see Chapter 9 for suggestions) or having them read a story about bullying. Then follow this up with a class discussion. Consider seating your students in a circle so that everyone can see each other. While you will want to encourage discussion, begin by making some key points, including the following:

- Describe what is meant by bullying, perhaps offering examples.
- Make it clear that bullying behavior of any kind is unacceptable and not permitted in school. In addi-

tion, you might state an underlying value, namely, that all children deserve to be treated with respect.

- When you describe to your students your classroom rules, make sure that "No bullying" is among them. (You might post these rules next to the clock so your students see them often.)
- Inform your students what they should do if they are bullied or they see a classmate being bullied.
- Tell your students that you will take reports of bullying seriously and there will be consequences for students who engage in these behaviors.

After you have made these points, engage your students in a discussion appropriate to their grade level to help them understand how bullying can be hurtful. Some topics you might discuss:

- You might ask them to talk about times they have been bullied (without mentioning names) and to describe how it felt. In this way you are helping to promote empathy, which is one of the keys to preventing bullying.
- Consider volunteering your own school experiences when you or a classmate was bullied.
- Ask your students why they think students engage in bullying. The reasons they offer may deter some students from acting in this way.
- Discuss the importance of supporting classmates who are targets of bullying, including informing an adult. This topic of empowering witnesses to bullying to take action is described later in this chapter.
- At the end of the discussion, tell your students that you are available to discuss any specific concerns they have privately. Tell them the best time to do this.

If you are not comfortable holding a classroom meeting, you may want to invite a guidance counselor or school psychologist to conduct the meeting with you. You may also want to attend a staff development workshop on this topic.

Role-play social situations with your students. You might do this at the class meeting. Consider having students assume the roles of bully, victim and bystander and give them common social situations where bullying might occur and have them act them out. The following are some social situations that you might have students role play:

- name calling
- cutting in front of a line
- taking the ball away from someone on the playground
- excluding a classmate during recess

After the role play, have your students talk about how they felt and what they might have said or done differently. In this way, students have a chance to try out their own responses and hear what their classmates might say and do. Give them feedback by having them consider whether their response is likely to get their point across without angering or provoking the other student. If you find that younger students are unable to role play these situations, you might act them out using puppets and then engage them in a discussion.

Closely monitor students who are at high risk for being bullied. Children are more prone to be bullied if they are withdrawn from their classmates, stand out in some way (for example, they are short, overweight or have an accent) attend special education programs, speak English as a second language or are new to the school.

Students who are isolated from their classmates are particularly vulnerable to being bullied. Stated another way, children are less likely to be bullied if they are actively involved with classmates, particularly during unstructured activities. You can lessen their chance of being a victim by helping them become more connected to and involved with their peers. As examples, you might integrate them into activities (especially on the playground), pair them with students who are likely to be accepting, and make sure they sit with other children during lunch.

Inform other school staff about potential bullying situations. If you become aware of a bullying incident in your classroom, make sure to inform other personnel, including special subject teachers and paraprofessionals, that come into contact with the students to monitor their behavior. This information will allow them to pay special attention to these students to ensure that no further incidents occur.

Present classroom lessons that have a bullying theme. You have a range of opportunities to integrate bullying into your academic lessons. Here are some examples:

- Read a book to your students about a child who is bullied (or if old enough have them read it aloud, taking turns) and then lead your students in a discussion of how a victim of bullying might feel, why bullies might behave that way, how the victim might respond to the bully, and how other children might help the victim. Books about bullying can be comforting to students who have been victims and can spark ideas how they might handle a social situation in the future. Chapter 9 has an extensive list of fiction and non-fiction books for children on bullying.

- After a discussion with your class about what bullying is and is not, present some scenarios to your students and ask them whether or not they meet the definition of bullying.

- Have your upper elementary or middle school class design a survey about bullying and then have your students complete it anonymously. Have them tally the results and present them in the form of bar graphs, using percentages. In addition to raising their awareness about bullying, this will help them practice and apply their math skills in a way that is meaningful to them.

- Draw a large picture of a child on the blackboard. Then ask your students to describe the characteristics of a bully as you write them on the picture. This exercise will help to communicate what is appropriate and inappropriate behavior and also convey what children think of bullies in the hope that it will discourage potential bullies.

Closely supervise areas where bullying is likely. As discussed previously, bullying often takes place in areas of the school that have minimal supervision such as the playground, the lunchroom, the bathroom, and even the back of the classroom. While some of these areas are outside of your control, you can help prevent bullying by being especially vigilant and visible during less structured activities. As an example, if you are a middle-school teacher, you may be able to deter bullying in the hallway by standing in your classroom doorway as students are changing classes. Similarly you need to scan your classroom regularly during unstructured activities to detect possible peer problems.

Encourage bystanders to bullying to take action. While you may not always observe bullying incidents, the likelihood is that some of your students will. These witnesses can thus play a valuable role in reducing bullying behavior. They can do this by telling the bully to stop what he is doing, by distracting the bully by getting him to focus on something else, by reaching out to the victim in friendship or support, and most importantly by informing a school staff member. Tell them that doing nothing is saying to the bully that it is okay to hurt other students. Also make the point that if they laugh at the bully's behavior or go along with what he is doing, they are contributing to the bullying.

Because students may be reluctant to inform an adult for fear they will be seen as a tattletale, it is important to stress to them that telling an adult about bullying is vastly different from tattling on a student. You might make the point that telling is what you do to get someone out of trouble and tattling is what you do to get someone in trouble. Also tell them that if they do come to you with a report of bullying that you will keep their name anonymous. One way of doing this is to have a box in your classroom where students can deposit notes about any concerns they have. It is better if the box is not restricted to issues of bullying so that students submitting bullying concerns cannot be identified.

Dealing with Bullying Incidents

No matter how diligent you are in trying to prevent bullying, incidents are likely to happen. If they do, you can take various steps to deal with these incidents to avoid their spinning out of control. Some of these strategies are discussed below:

Know your school's bullying policies. In deciding how to respond to an incident, make sure to review your school's policies and procedures for dealing with bullying. They may be contained in the school's code of conduct or in a separate document. If you have trouble finding them, check with the principal.

Take reports of bullying seriously. Follow up on all reports of bullying, even those that appear minor. Bear in mind that an incident may appear small to you but may loom large to the student. Make sure not to dismiss the incident with a "boys will be boys" attitude or tell the victim of bullying that he must fight his own battles. Assess the student's degree of distress and factor in your knowledge of his reactions in determining how to respond. Be especially attentive to students who come to you who are shy.

Act quickly. If you learn that a student is being emotionally or physically harassed, take immediate action to ensure his safety and security. The longer the abuse goes on, the greater the emotional impact on the student. Putting an immediate end to this behavior is important not only to protect the student but also to send a message to your other students that you will not tolerate this behavior and will do whatever is necessary to ensure your classroom is a safe haven.

Try to deal with the problem privately. Whether dealing with the bully or the victim, try to avoid a public airing of the issue. The victim may feel humiliated by having the bullying discussed in front of his peers while the bully may feel the need to escalate his aggressive behavior if he is challenged by the teacher in front of his classmates so that he does not "lose face." This may give rise to a public power struggle that can easily spiral out of control.

Inform the principal. This is particularly important if the incident is serious or ongoing. He or she will likely want to contact the parents of both the bully and the victim and may also want to take some disciplinary action with the bully. The principal may also want to inform other school staff such as the guidance counselor and paraprofessionals involved with the students.

Support the victim. Ask the student who was bullied what happened and then listen sympathetically to his response, making sure to convey that you take his concern seriously and understand his distress. Reassure him that he did the right thing by talking with you and that he is not to blame for the bullying. Emphasize that the bully was the one who behaved inappropriately. Let him know that you may need to inform other staff of the bullying but that the school will do its best to ensure the bullying does not happen again. Encourage the child to tell you of future bullying incidents and make sure to respond assertively if he does. If it appears that the child was being bullied in part because he is isolated from peers, help him connect with and befriend classmates.

Help the victim develop coping skills. If time allows, you may want to help the student develop effective ways of responding to the bully. In particular, you may want to teach him how to assert himself with the bully without being aggressive. The goal here is to help the student project a greater air of confidence without dissolving in tears but also without incurring the wrath of the bully. Towards this end, consider role-playing with him, suggesting what he might say or do to deflect the taunting. Often the best response of a student who is being taunted is to give a brief but direct "I-message" such as "I don't like what you're saying and I want you to stop" and then walk away. If he can respond this way, he is less likely to be targeted in the future. Chapter 7 gives some other examples of what the student might say. While the victim may be able to defuse the bullying with these strategies, it is critical that he understand that he is not responsible for resolving the bullying problem and that he should not hesitate to seek help from an adult if these strategies do not work.

Try to connect with the bully. You will likely want to discipline bullies in some way. Strategies and options for disciplining students who bully are presented in Chapter 4 and should be discussed with the principal. But just as the bully needs discipline, he also needs support and guidance. You may find that a sympathetic, understanding approach may elicit kinder, gentler behavior from the student. Try taking the bully aside and talking with him in a non-threatening manner. Listen attentively without condoning his behaviors. And as you do, try to find out what motivated his behavior. It may be that he wrongly perceived hostility from the other student. Or that he was trying to gain status with his peers. Once you can identify what was behind his bullying, try to provide appropriate guidance and emotional support such as offering other explanations for the victim's behavior or helping the bully learn how to obtain attention from peers in more appropriate ways. Ask him how else he might have responded while offering some suggestions of your own.

Monitor the situation. A student who has engaged in bullying is likely to do it again. Similarly a student who has been bullied is at risk for being victimized by other students. As a result, it is important for you to pay close attention to students who have been bullied and those who have done the bullying, and you may want to ask other staff to do the same. Make sure to check in with the victim periodically to find out if he is experiencing any further bullying. Let both the bully and the victim know that you and other school staff will be monitoring the situation closely. Their awareness of your vigilance will help to discourage the bully from tormenting his classmates and provide some comfort to the victim.

Chapter 6
The Role of the
Paraprofessional/Teacher Aide

Bullying often takes place in less structured and less supervised areas of the school. This includes such areas as the playground, lunchroom, bathroom, hallway and bus stop. These are precisely the areas where paraprofessionals are assigned, making your role critical in detecting and preventing bullying. Just as students need assurance that teachers will take bullying seriously and take steps to protect them in the classroom, so too they need reassurance that they will be protected in areas of the school supervised by paraprofessionals.

In this chapter we will examine the problem of bullying from the perspective of paraprofessionals, who may be called teacher aides or teaching assistants in some school districts. We will describe signs you can look for that suggest that a student is being bullied. And we will talk about what you can do as paraprofessionals to both prevent bullying and respond to incidents should they occur.

Warning Signs of Bullying

Recognizing and responding to bullying can be a real challenge for school staff, including paraprofessionals. First of all, it is unrealistic to expect that you as a parapro- fessional can notice or respond to every possible bullying incident that occurs in your assigned area, especially if you are supervising a large number of students. Second, bullies are often adept at targeting other children when adults are not present. Third, victims of bullying often fail to report incidents to school staff because they are not confident the school will take their concerns seriously or they fear retali- ation. As a result, bullying is a problem that often escapes detection by school staff.

Because of these obstacles in detecting bullying, it is critical that you as a paraprofessional be alert for signs that a child is being bullied. While you may not see the actual incident, you may see the results of the bullying through the behaviors of the victim. Here are some warning signs that may suggest that a student has been the target of bullying:

- withdrawal from peers
- unusual sadness
- frequent absence from school
- avoidance of certain school areas or activities
- not eating lunch
- playing alone on the playground
- frequent visits to the school nurse
- staying by the paraprofessional's side

What You Can Do to Prevent Bullying

The best way of dealing with bullying incidents is to prevent them from happening in the first place. Dan

Olweus, a Norwegian psychologist who is considered the world's leading researcher on bullying, has designed an anti-bullying program that has been implemented in many American schools and in some cases has brought about a 50 percent decline in bullying. A key premise of this program is that a comprehensive bullying prevention campaign must include all school staff if it is to have maximum impact. This includes paraprofessionals who are often the supervising adults present when bullying incidents take place. In this section we discuss some steps you can take to prevent bullying.

Be vigilant. Much like a lifeguard, a paraprofessional needs to continually scan the playground or cafeteria to detect possible problems. This makes your physical positioning critical so you can see as much of the area as possible. As you scan the area, keep a close watch on high-risk students, namely those who have a history of bullying or being bullied. You might want to carry a clipboard with you while on the playground or in the cafeteria to record bullying incidents.

Monitor hot spots. No matter how vigilant you are, you cannot keep all students in sight all the time. Within the areas that you supervise there may be spots or hidden corners that are sometimes hard for you to see but may be common bullying sites. For example, on the playground, bullying might take place behind a building or tree or at the far end of the playground. It is important to patrol these out of the way areas regularly. This may mean making the rounds of these areas on a random, unpredictable basis. If there are areas that are particularly inaccessible and thus hard to monitor, you may want to tell students to avoid these areas or even make them off-limits.

If you are supervising an area with another paraprofessional, you may want to work out a plan with her so that you are canvassing as much of the area as possible. In this way you are minimizing the areas where bullying can take place. The least effective strategy for ensuring maximum coverage is for two paraprofessionals to stand next to each other.

Identify patterns. Make note of patterns of bullying and use this information to recommend changes. For example, if you observe that most bullying incidents are taking place on the playground during a period when older and younger students are present, you might suggest to the principal or playground supervisor that older and younger children be separated.

Encourage bystanders to report incidents of bullying. Because you cannot see all incidents of bullying that take place on your watch, you want to encourage students to report incidents to you or another school staff member. Help them understand that telling about bullying is not the same as tattling on a student. You might point out that telling is what you do to get someone out of trouble and tattling is what you do to get someone in trouble. If students do inform you about a bullying incident, make sure to keep their names confidential and praise them for coming forward.

Keep a watchful eye on isolated students. Children who are loners are prime candidates for being bullied. Put another way, students are less likely to be bullied if they are with another child. What this means is that you can lessen their chance of being bullied by helping them become more involved with their peers. As examples, you might orchestrate their participation in playground activities and make sure they do not eat lunch alone.

Provide activities for students during recess. Students are more likely to engage in bullying when they are bored and do not have other activities to occupy them. Offer activities that grab their attention and also serve as an outlet for their energy.

Make available alternative activities to at-risk children. While most students opt for physical activities during recess, make sure to provide items for students who prefer quieter or non-competitive activities such as board games, books and art materials. Through these activities they may develop relationships with other students that will make them less of a target for bullies.

What to Do When Bullying Happens

Despite your best efforts to prevent bullying, incidents will no doubt happen. Let's take a look at some key steps you can take when they do:

Make sure you understand your school's bullying policies and procedures. Many schools have written policies about how to handle bullying. They may be found in the school's code of conduct or may be in a separate document. Get a hold of this information and be sure you understand what is expected of you when an incident happens.

Respond quickly to all reports of bullying. Keep in mind that an incident may seem small to you but may loom large to the student. Responding immediately and assertively is critical not only to protect the victim but also to let other students know that bullying will not be tolerated on your watch. The longer the bullying goes on, the greater the emotional impact on the victim. So do not delay in taking action.

Support the victim. It is important that you convey to the victim that you take his concern seriously. Ask what happened and then listen sympathetically to his response. Reassure him that he did nothing wrong and is not at fault for the bullying. Make sure that he understands that the bully was the one who behaved inappropriately not him. Let him know that you will need to inform other school staff of the incident so they can take action with the bully to ensure the bullying does not happen again. Encourage the victim to tell you of future incidents and make sure to respond assertively if he does. You may also want to help the student learn how to be assertive with bullies but make sure he knows not to respond physically. If time allows, try role-playing with him, suggesting what he might do or say to project a greater air of confidence. These strategies are discussed in greater detail in Chapter 4.

Discipline the student but avoid harsh measures. While your first priority is to make sure that the bullying has stopped, you may also want to discipline the bully to deter future incidents. Make sure that whatever consequences you provide are consistent with school policy. If you are not sure what steps you are allowed to take, check with an administrator. Some steps you might consider, if consistent with school policy, include sitting the child down during an activity, prohibiting him from an activity on subsequent days, sending him to the principal's office or informing the principal at the end of the activity. Keep in mind, however, that your goal is to stop the bullying rather than to humiliate the student. Towards this end, you want to make sure not to bully the bully and thus you want to avoid harsh disciplinary measures, which may only fuel the bully's anger and make him more determined to continue his bullying.

Connect with the bully. At the same time that you are disciplining the student, you may also want to provide him with guidance. Bear in mind that bullies bully for a reason, whether to gain status with their peers, to exert power over them, to punish another child, or to vent frustration with problems at home or in school. Your goal here is to identify what emotional needs underlie the bullying and then provide appropriate emotional support. For example, you may conclude that the bully needs help gaining attention from peers in more appropriate ways.

Providing this guidance does not require a degree in psychology. But it does require establishing some trust with the child. You might try taking him aside and talking with him in a non-threatening manner. Listen attentively but make sure not to condone his behavior. Through some probing questioning, you might be able to elicit what motivated his actions. You may find that a sympathetic, understanding approach such as this may elicit kinder, gentler behavior from the student.

Monitor the students. In the days and weeks following the incident, pay special attention to the bully as well as the victim and let both students know that you and other staff will be doing this. Walk past the bully often to let him know that you are monitoring him carefully. Also check in periodically with the victim to find out if the bully is leaving him alone.

Chapter 7
The Role of the Parents

As parents you may experience considerable distress upon hearing that your child is being bullied. This concern is usually well-founded. Being bullied can be a painful and in some cases devastating experience for children.

While the chief responsibility for preventing school bullying lies with school staff, you also play a key role in this effort by being alert to possible signs of bullying and acting assertively if you learn it is occurring. If your child is being bullied, this means providing him with emotional support and guidance. If your child is the one doing the bullying, this means taking a firm stand with him to stop his aggressive behavior but also providing him with guidance in response to the underlying reasons for his behavior. In both cases, you will want to work closely with the school to ensure that the bullying stops immediately and no further incidents occur.

Children need assurance that their parents as well as school staff will respond seriously to bullying incidents and take steps to protect them. Bullying is not a problem that you can afford to ignore. The stakes are simply too high for you to leave this problem in the hands of your child to re-solve. In this chapter we will take a close-up look at practical steps you can take to ensure that the ordeal of bullying ends as soon as possible.

Signs that Your Child May Be a Victim of Bullying

Just as school staff may be unaware that bullying is occurring, so too you may be unaware that your child is being bullied. Children are often hesitant to tell their parents that a classmate is bothering them, either because they are humiliated about the bullying or because they are afraid that their parents' response may make the problem worse. As a result, you will need to be vigilant for clues from their be-havior signaling that they are anxious or upset. Children who are targets of bullying often display signs of distress through changes in their behavior. Trust your instincts. You know your children better than anyone else and are in a good position to recognize when something is amiss.

Here are some of the more common signs that may suggest that your child is being bullied:

- often develops a stomachache or headache in the morning
- is resistant to going to school
- is fearful of walking to or from school, or riding the school bus
- frequently asks for or takes money beyond his normal needs
- is receiving lower grades than usual
- appears withdrawn, upset or tearful after school
- comes home from school with torn clothes or unex-plained bruises

- is unusually hungry after school (because his lunch money was stolen)
- is missing some of his belongings
- seems isolated from his peers
- has been unusually moody and quick to anger
- has been acting aggressively towards other children
- has been having problems sleeping or eating
- talks of or attempts suicide

What to Do If Your Child is Being Bullied

Learning that your child is being bullied may engender strong emotional reactions. You may respond by pressuring your child to stand up to the bully and if necessary retaliate physically. Or you may storm angrily into school demanding to know what they are doing about it. Or you may confront the parents of the bully. These responses rarely help and in most cases make the problem worse. But you are far from helpless in addressing this problem. Consider taking the following steps if you learn that your child is being bullied by a classmate:

Encourage your child to tell you and school staff if he is being bullied. In light of the prevalence of bullying, it is a good practice for all parents to tell their children to inform them or a school adult if a child is bothering them. In this way you are conveying to your child that he is not solely responsible for dealing with bullying. Help your child understand the difference between reporting an incident, which is intended to protect himself, and tattling, which is intended to get someone into trouble.

Get up to speed on cyberbullying. It used to be that home was a safe haven for children from the cruelties of peer pressure. But with technology this has all changed. Children may now intimidate or harass their peers through their computer or even their cell phone. While this form of remote bullying can be just as distressing to children as the more direct forms of bullying, parents are often unaware it is taking place. If children are receiving nasty messages from their peers, they are unlikely to let their parents know, fearful that they will be barred from going online. Don't wait for your child to come to you with concerns about cyberbullying. Instead, take the initiative by talking with him about what to do if he is receiving upsetting messages on the Internet. Encourage him to let you know and tell him not to respond to the bully online. Also suggest that he keep personal information, including pictures and passwords, to himself.

Treat your child's reports of bullying seriously. If your child tells you that another child has been bothering him, take his concern seriously even if it appears minor to you. Remember that an incident may seem small to you but loom large to your child. Listen attentively and tell him that he did the right thing by talking with you. Inform him that he is not to blame for the bullying and be careful of making comments that suggest he did something wrong. Reassure him that you will do everything you can to make sure the bullying stops and that he will not have to deal with the problem alone. Tell him that you will need to speak with the school in order to deal with the bullying, but reassure him that this will help resolve the problem rather than make it worse. Do not delay in taking action. The longer the bullying goes on, the greater the emotional impact on your child.

Inform school staff promptly. At a minimum you should inform the teacher and principal of the bullying, but you may also want to involve other school staff, including the guidance counselor. You want to be forceful in insisting that the school deal with the bullying immediately, but you want to make sure that you are not so assertive as to alienate the school officials whose cooperation you will likely need to resolve the problem. Ideally, you will want to meet with school staff face to face to express your concerns and then work with them to develop a plan for ending the bullying and providing support to your child.

Don't stop there, however. Follow up your meeting with a letter to the teacher and principal thanking them for their support and summarizing the steps to be taken. Contact the school after a few days to find out if the bullying has stopped and of course also check with your child. If the bullying is continuing, consider scheduling another meeting with the school. Continue to advocate until you are confident the bullying has ended.

If you find that the school is not taking your concern seriously, consider contacting the superintendent. You might also take your child to his doctor and get a letter from the physician documenting your child's distress and requesting that the school take immediate action to relieve the problem. It is also helpful in dealing with the school to keep a record of incidents that your child describes to you as well as your contacts with school officials and retain copies of letters you have written and received regarding the bullying.

Coach your child on how to respond to the bully. To begin with, tell your child what he should not do, and that is to retaliate against the bully or get in an angry exchange with him. This could result in your child getting hurt or the bully becoming more determined to torment your child. In addition, encouraging your child to retaliate is giving him the message that aggression is an appropriate response to a problem.

This does not mean, however, that your child is powerless to respond in the face of a bully. But you want to help him find a way of responding that defuses rather than enflames the situation. A bully thrives on upsetting his target as it gives him a feeling of power. So encourage your child to not let the bully see that he has upset him. The bully may aim his barbs elsewhere when he does not get the response he wants.

Depending on the situation, you might encourage your child to ignore the bully and walk away without appearing to be upset. Or you might help him learn to be more assertive by telling the bully to stop in a clear, firm, simple manner and then walk away. Walking away helps to ensure the incident does not escalate. You might suggest some one-line responses to your child and then have him practice saying them, perhaps even role-playing what your child encounters with the bully. Examples of responses are listed later in this chapter. While your child may be able to defuse the bullying with these strategies, it is important that he understand that he is not responsible for resolving the bullying problem and that he should not hesitate to seek help from an adult if these strategies do not work.

What should you do if your child fears being hurt by the bully if he does not give him what he wants? Tell him that he should opt for safety and protect himself by doing what the bully says, and then he should tell an adult. It is not worth getting hurt over a possession that can be replaced.

Help your child connect with his peers. Bullies tend to target children who are isolated from their peers. The more involved your child is with his classmates, the less likely he will be a target for bullies. If he tends to stay to himself in school, help him develop friendships with classmates by encouraging him to invite children over to your house. It is preferable that he invite one child at a time so there is no chance that he will be ganged up on or excluded. Also try to find some social activities that he is interested in joining. You might also speak with the teacher to encourage her to help your child build some friendships in school as well as have her suggest classmates whom he might invite over. In addition, consider asking the teacher to highlight your child's accomplishments, talents and interests in class to help give him some status among his peers.

Help your child project a confident air. Just as an isolated child is more likely to be a target of bullies, a child lacking in confidence has a greater chance of being a victim. Help your child appear confident by encouraging him to hold his head high, make eye contact with others and walk with confidence. If he can do this, the bully will be less likely to single him out.

What Your Child Might Say to the Bully

Your child may not know what to do or say when faced with a bully's taunting. You might want to help him develop some responses in advance that may serve to diffuse the bully's anger or encourage him to leave your child alone. These do not need to be lengthy rejoinders or clever retorts and they certainly should not be confrontational. The idea is for your child to have something to say so that he does not dissolve in tears or appear vulnerable. Have him rehearse these responses at home. As he does, encourage him to speak confidently, look the bully in the eye and then walk away. Here are some examples of what your child might say:

- Say "no" or "stop it" in a firm manner and then walk away.

- Respond with a short and simple phrase (for example, "That's your opinion" or "Whatever you say") and then walk away.
- Use a direct and concise I-message (for example, "That's my ball and I want it back").
- Ask the bully to repeat what he said in an effort to take the wind out of his sails.
- Tell the bully "Come to think of it, you're right" and then walk away.
- Ask the bully an innocent question (for example, "Why are you saying these mean things about me? I've never done anything to you.").
- Appeal to the bully's desire for peer status (for example, "Saying mean things to kids is a pretty nerdy thing to do").
- Say something unpredictable that may confuse the bully (for example, "If you tell me what I did to you, I'll say I'm sorry").
- Try to disarm the bully by using humor (for example, "That's the nicest thing anybody's ever said to me").
- Reach out to the bully (for example, "Let's not argue. Do you want to play a game with me?").

Helping Your Child Avoid Bullying

Sometimes the best way to deal with a bully is to figure out how to stay away from him. While it is not fair that your child may need to go out of his way to avoid contact with a bully, doing this may spare him considerable distress and anxiety. Have your child describe to you precisely the circumstances of the bullying. Then brainstorm with him some ways of minimizing contact with the bully. Some avoidance strategies are offered below:

- Have your child take a different route to or from school, or leave a little earlier to avoid meeting up with the bully. You might also consider driving him or having him walk with older children.
- Have your child sit near the bus driver on the school bus.
- If your child is being bullied on the bus, let the bus driver know so he can monitor the situation. Suggest that he assign seats to the children, with the bully placed far away from your child.
- Do not allow your child to bring expensive items or excess money to school.
- Have your child take a different route to his classes if he is being harassed in the hallway.
- Have your child avoid areas of the school that are unsupervised or situations where he is isolated from classmates.
- As a last resort, request a change of schedule for your child. Or, better yet, insist that the bully's schedule be changed.

What to Do If Your Child is the Bully

If you are informed that your child is bullying a classmate, take this information seriously. Do not dismiss this concern because you believe this is just kids being kids. Children who bully are prone to problems in later years. Here are some steps that you might take:

Meet with the principal or teacher. In addition to getting their observations, you may also want to speak to other staff who observed your child such as playground and cafeteria aides or the bus driver. The more information you can get about your child's behavior, the better able you are to figure out what he did and why he did it.

Take a hard line on bullying. If you conclude after talking with school staff that your child has been bullying a classmate, speak with your child. Convey to him in no uncertain terms that bullying in any form is unacceptable and must stop immediately. In talking with him, you might label his behavior as bullying so that he understands that his behavior is distinct from fooling around. Tell him that you will be in frequent contact with the school about his behavior and take seriously any further reports that he is hurting or causing distress to other children.

Try to understand your child's behavior and respond accordingly. Children bully for a reason, whether to gain peer approval, to exert power over them, to punish a child, or to vent frustration with problems at home or in school. You need to try to get to the source of what motivated your child's behavior. In addition to asking him the obvious question, namely, "why did you behave that way?," you might also ask whether he felt someone had done something to him or whether something was upsetting him. The behavior of bullies is often fueled by social misperceptions.

If you can identify the emotional source of your child's behavior, try to address it in such a way that he does not feel the need to bully. You might suggest to him how he might have handled the situation differently without resorting to verbal or physical aggression, and how he might handle social situations in the future. You might even role-play if he is receptive. Also try to promote your child's empathy by helping him understand how a child who was bullied might feel. Consider telling him that his behavior will cause other children to avoid him out of fear.

If the bullying continues, arrange a consequence that is in proportion to the severity of his actions, but do not humiliate or embarrass him. Also do not use physical discipline as this reinforces the message that "might makes right."

Work with the school to modify his behavior. The school may want to take some disciplinary measures. If these consequences seem reasonable and calculated to deter future behavior rather than just punish your child, let your child know that you agree with the school's discipline. If your child's behavior was an expression of anger, you might ask if the school has a place he can go or a person he can see when he is angry and prone to lash out at a peer. Also encourage his teacher to find ways to reward or praise your child when he engages in appropriate school behavior, particularly acts of kindness or helpfulness towards his peers. You may even want to set up a behavior modification system in which your child can earn material rewards for kind or helpful behavior either at home or in school.

Monitor your child's media exposure. Pay attention to the television shows he watches and the video and computer games he plays and do not hesitate to limit his exposure to media violence. Research indicates that viewing violent programs or playing violent games can actually give rise to aggressive behavior.

Pay close attention to your child's social behavior. Take note of whom he spends time with, where he goes and what he does. Set reasonable curfews and restrict him from places, activities and children that you perceive to be bad influences and may be contributing to his bullying behavior.

If your child continues to bully despite efforts to modify his behavior, seek help from a counselor. You might discuss the problem with the school psychologist or seek help from a mental health professional. Your community may have a mental health center that provides counseling services at relatively low cost.

Chapter 8
Bullying: A Call to Action

It is not an exaggeration to say that bullying is the foremost mental health challenge faced by schools today. It is a problem that affects the entire student body. The students who are doing the bullying are prone to serious problems later in life, including job-related difficulties, relationship problems and criminal behavior. The students who are their victims may suffer psychological pain that continues long after the bullying ends. They may experience anxiety, low self-esteem, depression and in some cases even suicidal thoughts. And the students who observe the bullying—the bystanders—may go through school in a constant state of fear, afraid that they will be the next victims.

The problem of bullying thus demands nothing short of the full attention of educators. It is a challenge that schools must confront foursquare. Students need assurance that schools will view bullying seriously and take vigorous measures to safeguard all children. School staff must send a strong message that bullying is unacceptable and that they will be vigilant in detecting bullying and will respond seriously if they become aware of its occurrence.

Fortunately bullying is a concern that schools can do something about if they are willing to recognize its serious consequences and confront by committing the necessary school resources. As we have seen from the program outlined in Chapter 3, schools have at their disposal a variety of strategies they can use to both prevent bullying from happening and to deal with incidents when they do happen.

These strategies are most effective when they are part of a comprehensive bullying prevention program that is implemented at the district, school and classroom levels. The program must be comprehensive in the true sense of the word. It must encompass all school staff but it also needs the support and commitment of parents and students. In addition, interventions with students should not be limited to bullies or victims. Other students—the bystanders—can help prevent bullying by learning to take action when they witness incidents.

Schools that are willing to invest the necessary resources in the planning and implementation of a bullying prevention program are likely to be rewarded in the form of a decrease in bullying incidents. In addition, they may see a decline in other anti-social behaviors such as vandalism, fighting, theft and truancy.

A bullying prevention program will have minimal impact, however, if it is implemented and then abandoned. Bullying prevention is not a one-shot deal. For this kind of program to be most effective, it must be ongoing. This means that schools must revisit this issue every year. It also means they must regularly evaluate the degree to which bullying incidents are continuing. In short, the program will have the greatest impact when it is woven into the fabric of the school culture.

Yet despite the pervasiveness of bullying and the strategies available for its prevention, schools have often been reluctant to implement bullying prevention programs. Some administrators may feel that their school staff are already overburdened with program initiatives. Others may hesitate to offer such a program for fear that the public will perceive that their school has a problem with bullying. Still others may not see the need for a program, viewing bullying as a natural part of childhood that can even have the benefit of building character.

These are obstacles, however, that can be overcome with efficient planning, effective education and good communication. The problem of bullying is simply too serious and too widespread for us to give in to these concerns. Bullying is not a problem that will go away if ignored.

Chapter 9
Bullying Resources

Printed Material for Adults

Adams, H. Peace in the Classroom: Practical Lessons in Living for Elementary-Age Children. Winnepeg, MB: Peguis, 1994.

Aftab, P. The Parent's Guide to Protecting Your Children in Cyberspace. New York: McGraw-Hill, 2000.

Alexander, J. Bullying : Practical and Easy-To-Follow Advice. New York: Element Books, 1998.

Beane, A. L. The Bully Free Classroom: Over 100 Tips and Strategies for Teachers K – 8. Minneapolis: Free Spirit, 1999.

Beaudoin, M., and Taylor, M. Breaking the Culture of Bullying and Disrespect, Grades K-8: Best Practices and Successful Strategies. Thousand Oaks, CA: Corwin Press, 2004.

Bodine, R. J., Crawford, D. K., and Schrumpf, F. Creating the Peaceable School: A Comprehensive Program for Teaching Conflict Resolution. (2nd ed.) Champaign, IL: Research Press, 2004.

Borba, Michelle. No More Misbehavin'. New York, NY: John Wiley & Sons, 2003.

Borba, Michelle. Building Moral Intelligence. New York, NY: John Wiley & Sons, 2001.

Borba, Michelle. Nobody Likes Me, Everyone Hates Me. New York, NY: John Wiley & Sons, 2005.

Bosse, Arthur. Designing Effective Youth Prevention Programming. Addiction, March, 2005.

Cohen, J., & Elias, M. School Climate: Building Safe, Supportive and Engaging Classrooms & Schools (laminated reference guide). Port Chester, NY: Dude Publishing, 2011.

Coloroso, B. The Bully, the Bullied, and the Bystander: From Preschool to High School—How Parents and Teachers Can Help Break the Cycle of Violence. New York: Harper Resource, 2004.

Conn, K. Bullying and Harassment: A Legal Guide for Educators. Alexandria, VA: Association for Supervision and Curriculum Development, 2004.

Cooper, S. Sticks and Stones: Seven Ways Your Child Can Deal with Teasing, Conflict and Other Hard Times. New York: Random House, 2000.

Crone, Deanne & Horner, Robert. Building Positive Behavior Support Systems in Schools. New York, NY: Guilford Press, 2003.

Davis. S. Schools Where Everyone Belongs: Practical Strategies for Reducing Bullying. Champaign, IL: Research Press, 2005.

Dellasega, C., and Nixon, C. Girl Wars: 12 Strategies That Will End Female Bullying. New York: Fireside, 2003.

DeRoche, Edward. Character Matters: In Classrooms, at School, at Home (laminated reference guide). Port Chester, NY: Dude Publishing, 2008.

Ditrano, C. Functional Behavioral Assessments (FBA) and Behavioral Intervention Plans (BIP) (laminated reference guide). Port Chester, NY: Dude Publishing, 2010.

Duncan, N. Sexual Bullying: Gender Conflict and Pupil Culture in Secondary Schools. London: Routledge, 1999.

Dunkelblau, Ed. Social, Emotional and Character Development (SECD) for Teachers, for Students, for Parents (laminated reference guide). Port Chester, NY: Dude Publishing, 2009.

Eastman, M., and Rozen, S.C. Taming the Dragon in Your Child: Solutions for Breaking the Cycle of Family Anger. New York: John Wiley & Sons, 1994.

Espelage, D. L., and Swearer, S. M. (eds.) Bullying in American Schools: A Socio-Ecological Perspective on Prevention and Intervention. Mahwah, NJ: Lawrence Erlbaum Associates, 2004.

Freedman, J. S. Easing the Teasing: Helping Your Child Cope with Name-Calling, Ridicule, and Verbal Bullying. New York: McGraw Hill, 2002.

Fried, S., and Fried, P. Bullies & Victims: Helping Your Child Survive the Schoolyard Battlefield. New York: M. Evans & Co., 1996.

Garrity, C., Baris, M., and Porter, W. Bully-Proofing Your Child: A Parent's Guide. Longmont, CO: Sopris West, 2000.

Garrity, C., Jens, K., Porter, W., Sager, N., and Short-Camilli, C. Bully-Proofing Your School: A Comprehensive Approach for Elementary Schools. (2nd ed.) Longmont, CO: Sopris West, 2000.

Giannetti, C., and Sagarese, M. Cliques: 8 Steps to Help Your Child Survive the Social Jungle. New York: Broadway Books, 2001.

Girard, K., and Koch, S. Conflict Resolution in the Schools: A Manual for Educators. San Francisco: Jossey-Bass, 1996.

Gralla, P., & Kinkoph, S. The Complete Idiot's Guide to Protecting Your Child Online. Indianapolis, IN: Que, 2000.

Greenbaum, S., and Turner, B. Set Straight on Bullies. Westlake Village, CA: National School Safety Center, 1989.

Hinduja, S., and Patchin, J.W. Bullying Beyond the School-yard: Preventing and Responding to Cyberbullying. Thousand Oaks, CA: Corwin Press, 2008.

Hinduja, S., and Patchin, J.W. Cyberbullying: Identification, Prevention and Response (laminated reference guide). Port Chester, NY: Dude Publishing, 2011.

Hoover, J. H., and Oliver, R. Bullying Prevention Handbook: A Guide for Principals, Teachers, and Counselors. Bloomington, IND: National Educational Service, 1996.

Huggins, P., and Shakarian, L. Helping Kids Handle Put-Downs. Longmont, CO: Sopris West, 1998.

Hurst, Marianne D. When It Comes to Bullying, There Are No Boundaries. Education Week, February 9, 2005.

Janney, Rahcel & Snell, M. Teachers' Guide to Inclusive Practices: Behavioral Support. Touson, MD: Brookes Publishing Co., 2003.

Juvonen, J. Peer Harassment in Schools. New York, NY: Guilford Press, 2000.

Karres, E. V. S. Violence-Proof Your Kids Now: How to Recognize the 8 Warning Signs and What To Do About Them. Berkeley, CA: Conari Press, 2000.

Kenworthy, Tom & O'Driscoll, Patrick. Red Lake Community Shaken by 'Darkest Day.' USA Today, March 23, 2005.

Kowalski, R.M., Limber, S.P., and Agatston, P.W. Cyber Bullying: Bullying in the Digital Age. Victoria, Australia: Blackwell Publishing, 2008.

Liebson, Richard. Students Taught How to Combat "Cyberbullying." The Journal News, February 9, 2005.

Limber, Susan. What Works—and Doesn't Work—in Bullying Prevention and Intervention. Student Assistance Journal, Winter, 2004.

Marano, H. E. Why Doesn't Anybody Like Me? A Guide to Raising Socially Confident Kids. New York: William Morrow and Co., 1998.

McConnel Fad, Kathleen & Patton, James R. Behavioral Intervention Planning (Revised Edition). Austin, TX: Pro-Ed, Inc., 2000.

McCoy, E. What to Do When Kids Are Mean to Your Child. Pleasantville, NY: Readers Digest, 1997.

McNamara, B., and McNamara, F. Keys to Dealing with Bullies. Hauppauge, NY: Barron's Educational Series, 1997.

Olweus, D. Bullying at School: What We Know and What We Can Do. Malden, MA: Blackwell Publishers, 1994.

Osher, D. Dwyer, K., & Jackson, S. Safe, Supportive & Successful Schools: Step by Step. Longmont, CO: Sopris West, 2003.

Rhode, G., Jenson, W.R., and Reavis, H.K. The Tough Kid Book: Practical Classroom Management Strategies. Longmont, CO: Sopris West, 1992.

Ross, D. M. Childhood Bullying, Teasing, and Violence: What School Personnel, Other Professionals, and Parents Can Do. (2nd ed.) Annapolis Junction, MD: American Counseling Association, 2003.

Scott, S. How to Say No and Keep Your Friends: Peer Pressure Reversal for Teens and Preteens. (2nd ed.) Amherst, MA: Human Resource Development Press, 1997.

Shariff, S. Confronting Cyber-Bullying: What Schools Need to Know to Control Misconduct and Avoid Legal Consequences. Cambridge, UK: Cambridge University Press, 2009.

Shore, K. An Educator's Guide to Bullying Prevention (laminated reference guide). Port Chester, NY: Dude Publishing, 2011.

Shore, K. Elementary Teacher's Discipline Problem Solver. San Francisco: Jossey-Bass, 2003.

Shore, K. Keeping Kids Safe. Paramus, NJ: Prentice Hall Press, 2001.

Shore, K. Special Kids Problem Solver: Ready-to-Use Interventions for Helping All Students with Academic, Behavioral & Physical Problems. Paramus, NJ: Prentice Hall, 1998.

Siris, Karen & Osterman, Karen. Interrupting the Cycle of Bullying and Victimization in the Elementary Classroom. Phi Delta Kappan, December 2004, p. 288-291.

Sjostrom, L., and Stein, N. D. Bullyproof: A Teacher's Guide on Teasing and Bullying for Use with Fourth and Fifth Grade Students. Washington, DC: National Education Association, 1996.

Stern-LaRosa, C., and Bettmann, E. H. The Anti-Defamation League's Hate Hurts: How Children Learn and Unlearn Prejudice. New York: Scholastic, 2001.

Sullivan, K. The Anti-Bullying Handbook. New York: Oxford University Press, 2000.

Sullivan, M. Safety Monitor: How to Protect Your Kids Online. Santa Monica, CA: Bonus Books, 2002.

Swartz, Jon. Schoolyard Bullies Get Nastier Online. USA Today, March 7, 2005.

Thompson, M., Cohen, L. J., and Grace, C. O. Mom, They're Teasing Me: Helping Your Child Solve Social Problems. New York: Ballantine Books, 2002.

Thompson, M., Grace, C. O., and Cohen, L. J. Best Friends, Worst Enemies: Understanding the Social Lives of Children. New York: Ballantine Books, 2002.

Voors, W. The Parent's Book about Bullying: Changing the Course of Your Child's Life. Center City, MN: Hazelden, 2000.

Walker, H.M., Ramsey, E., & Greshman, F.M. Antisocial Behavior in Schools: Evidence Based Practices. Belmont, CA: Wadsworth, 2004.

Willard, N.E., and Steiner, K. Cyberbullying and Cyberthreats: Responding to the Challenge of Online Social Aggression, Threats, and Distress. Champaign, IL: Research Press, 2008.

Wiseman, R. Queen Bees & Wannabes: Helping Your Daughter Survive Cliques, Gossip, Boyfriends & Other Realities of Adolescence. New York: Crown Publishers, 2002.

Zarzour, K. Facing the Schoolyard Bully: How to Raise an Assertive Child in an Aggressive World. (2nd ed.) Buffalo, NY: Firefly Books, 2000.

Books for Children: Fiction

Akili. Marianthe's Story: Painted Words/Spoken Memories. New York: Greenwillow, 1998.

> Marianthe is an immigrant child who knows little English when she begins school in her new country. When she is teased by a classmate because of her struggles with the language, she discovers that she can communicate her family story by painting what she sees and feels.

Berenstain. S. The Berenstain Bears and the Bully. New York: Random House, 1993.

> Sister Bear learns to stand up to the tormenting behavior of a cub named Tuffy.

Berenstain. S., and Berenstain, J. The Berenstain Bears and Too Much Teasing. New York: Random House, 1995.

> Brother bear enjoys teasing his sister, but learns how hurtful ridicule can be when he becomes the target of teasing in school.

Blume, J. Blubber. New York: Simon-Schuster Children's Publishing, 2002.

> Jill torments a classmate named Linda about being overweight but comes to see the hurtfulness of her actions when she sees her friend ridiculed.

Bottner, B. Bootsie Barker Bites. Emeryville, CA: Penguin Group, 1992.

> Intended for preschool and young elementary students, this book tells a story in which girls fig-

ure out how to resolve a conflict with an aggressive playmate in a non-aggressive manner.

Brown, M. T. Arthur's April Fool. Boston: Little, Brown, 1985.

Arthur is scared that a classmate is going to make good on his threat to hurt him as he performs in a school assembly but he uses his cleverness to figure a way out.

Browne, A. Willy the Champ. New York: Candlewick Press, 2002.

Willy is not very good at sports but he deserves to be crowned champ when he outdoes the local bully.

Carlson, N. Loudmouth George and the Sixth-Grade Bully. Minneapolis: Carolrhoda Books, 2003.

George and his friend Harriet figure out a way to foil a bully and teach him a lesson he won't forget.

Coleman, M. Weirdo's War. New York: Orchard Books, 1998.

Daniel, a high school student, prefers sitting in the library doing math calculations to being with friends. When he goes on an excursion with classmates during spring break, he becomes the target of taunting and humiliation. He eventually forms an unlikely bond with his chief tormentor and they learn they need to work together to get by in school.

Cox, J. Mean Mean Maureen Green. New York: Random House Childrens' Books, 2001.

Lilly fears meeting up with a bully but with the aid of a classmate she conquers her fear and learns to stand up to mean mean Maureen Green.

Dadey, D. King of the Kooties. New York: Walker Publishing, 2001.

> Louisa, the class bully, tags the new kid in class as the "King of the Kooties," but Nate helps the new child figure out how to disarm the bully with their wits.

Friesen, G. Men of Stone. Toronto: Kids Can Press, 2000.

> A 15-year old boy who likes to dance is tormented by his peers but he learns to stand up to the bully while remaining true to himself and his passion.

Koss, A. The Girls. New York: Puffin Books, 2000.

> Maya, a middle-school student, is devastated when she is ostracized by members of her clique led by Candace who decides who's in and who's out.

McKeon, K. Baseball Ballerina Strikes Out. New York: Random House, 2000.

> A baseball-playing, ballet-dancing girl is subjected to teasing from classmates, but she hatches a scheme with her coach to teach them a lesson.

Moss, M. Amelia Takes Command. Middleton, WI: Pleasant Company, 1999.

> Fifth-grader Amelia is the target of the class bully, but she gains the courage to stand up for herself while spending a week at Space Camp.

Myers, C. Wings. New York: Scholastic Press, 2000.

> Ikarus Jackson is the target of ridicule at school because of his wings but he learns to celebrate his differences and embrace his individuality.

Polacco, P. Thank You, Mr. Falker. New York, Philomel Books, 1998.

> Trisha is a fifth-grader who faces the dual challenge of struggling with reading and dealing with the taunts of a bully. With the help of her teacher, she begins to conquer her reading problem and in the process discovers her artistic talent.

Sachar, L. There's a Boy in the Girls' Bathroom. New York: Random House, 1987.

> Bradley is a fifth-grade bully who is without friends and hard to like. With the help of a counselor and the friendship of a new boy in school, he learns to gain confidence, change his behaviors and make friends with his classmates.

Shange, N. Whitewash. New York: Walker and Co., 1997.

> While on her way home from school, Helene-Angel, an African American girl, and her brother, are attacked by three white boys. She learns that others care for her when her classmates come to her home to escort her to school. Based on a true incident, this book is an effective vehicle for promoting discussion about racially based bullying.

Van Draanen, W. Shredderman. New York: Knopf, 2004.

> Fifth-grader Nolan Byrd is tired of the relentless taunting he has received at the hands of a classmate. Determined to strike back, he hatches a plan to stop the bullying by using a secret identity: Shredderman.

White, E. B. Charlotte's Web. New York: HarperCollins, 1974.
E.B. White's enduring classic depicts the isolating consequences of bullying behavior and the important role that a friend can play in another's life.

Yep, L. Cockroach Cooties. New York: Hyperion, 2000.
Teddy and his younger brother learn that the school bully is scared of cockroaches so they concoct a plan to scare him. In the process they come to understand him better when they discover that his bullying behavior is the result of a difficult home life.

Books for Children: Non-Fiction

Agassi, M. Hands are Not for Hitting. Minneapolis: Free Spirit, 2000. (For grades preschool-1)

Appleman, D. Always Use Protection: A Teen's Guide to Safe Computing. Berkeley, CA: Apress, 2004.

Cohen-Posey, K. How to Handle Bullies, Teasers and Other Meanies: A Book that Takes the Nuisance Out of Name Calling and Other Nonsense. Highland City, FL: Rainbow Books, 1995. (For grades 4–7)

Johnston, M. Dealing with Bullying. Center City, MN: Hazelden, 1998. (For grades K-4)

Kaufman, G., Raphael, L., and Espeland, P. Stick Up for Yourself: Every Kid's Guide to Personal Power and Positive Self-Esteem. Minneapolis: Free Spirit Publishing, 1999. (For grades 3-7)

Miller, D. Time to Tell 'Em Off! A Pocket Guide to Overcoming Peer Ridicule. Merrifield, VA: Deanna Miller, 2002. (For grades 5-12)

Pike, K., Mumper, J., and Fiske, A. Teaching Kids to Care and Cooperate. New York: Scholastic, 2000. (For grades 2-5)

Powell, J. Talking About Bullying. Chicago: Raintree, 1999. (For grades 1-3)

Romain, T. Bullies Are a Pain in the Brain. Minneapolis: Free Spirit Publishing, 1997. (For grades 3-7)

Romain, T. Cliques, Phonies, & Other Baloney. Minneapolis: Free Spirit Publishing, 1998. (For grades 3-8)

Sanders, P. Bullying. Brookfield, CT: Copper Beech Books, 1996. (For ages 9-12)

Schwartau, W. Internet & Computer Ethics for Kids. Seminole, FL: Interpact Press, 2001.

Thomas, P., and Harker, L. Stop Picking On Me: A First Look at Bullying. Hauppauge, NY: Barron's Educational Series, 2000. (For ages 4-8)

Webster-Doyle, T. Why is Everybody Always Picking on Me? A Guide to Handling Bullies. New York: Weatherhill, 1997. (For ages 9-12)

Videos

Broken Toy is a 25-minute video from National Center for Youth Issues. It is for students in grades 4 to 6 from Lucky Duck Publishing that tells the story of a 12-year boy named Raymond who is the constant target of bullying. The bullies only begin to question their treatment of him when they go too far.

Buddy Learns About Bullying is a 13-minute video from Marco Products for students in grades kindergarten to 3. Discusses ways that students can avoid being bullied and presents exercises to promote classroom discussion.

Bullied, Battered and Bruised is a 55-minute video from the Canadian Broadcasting Corporation that examines the physical and psychological consequences of bullying through the words of children who have been victims. Discusses how two schools are dealing with bullying.

Bullies & Harassment On Campus is a 21-minute video from TMW Media Group for students in grades 8 to 12. Featuring interviews with teens, this program discusses ways that students can deal with harassment from peers.

Bully Dance is a 10-minute video from Bullfrog Films for students in grades 5 to 12. In this non-verbal animated film, a bully disturbs an entire community and forces its members to confront the issues of peer pressure and the imbalance of power underlying bullying. Study guide is included.

Bullying is a 15-minute video from Schlessinger Media for students in grades 5 to 12. Helps students learn to deal with bullying through the use of vignettes. Teacher guide is included.

Bullying and How to Handle It: A Video for 3rd & 4th grades is a 12-minute video from Hazelden Publishing & Educational Services. Elementary school students discuss their experiences with bullying and offer practical suggestions.

Bullying: Not Just a Guy Thing is a 30-minute video from AIMS Multimedia for students in grades 3 to 8. Tells the story of a girl bullied by middle-school girls and how she successfully deals with it.

Bullying: You Don't Have to Take it Anymore! Is a 23-minute video from Hourglass Productions for students in grades 7 to 12. It offers interviews with teenagers, dramatic scenarios, and expert advice in an effort to give pre-teens and teens the tools to deal with bullying.

Bully Smart is a 32-minute video from Tapeworm Video for students in grades 1 to 6. Hosted by the basketball star Kareem Abdul-Jabbar, this program offers various strategies for dealing with peer pressure and bullying.

Emily Breaks Free is a 15-minute animated video from Marsh Media for students in grades kindergarten to 4. Examines the issue of bullying from the perspective of a dog.

McGruff's Bully Alert is a 15-minute video from AIMS Multimedia for students in grades kindergarten to 5. Using the device of a dog named McGruff, this video shows students how to assert themselves in the presence of bullies.

Peer Pressure is a 30-minute video from Schlessinger Media for students in grades 5 to 9. Students talk candidly about the pressures they feel from their peers as well as ways to resist negative influences.

Push and Shove is a 25-minute animated video from Marco Products for students in grades 3 and 4. Presents a story that explores the feelings of both bully and victim.

Stop Bullying! Standing Up for Yourself and Others is a 20-minute video from Paraclete Press for teens. Using stories from teens about their own experiences with bullying, it depicts the painful impact of bullying and stresses the importance of taking action to defuse the bullying.

Sticks and Stones is a 17-minute video for students in grades 3 to 7 from the National Film Board of Canada in which children describe how it feels to be ridiculed when they come from families with non-traditional gender roles.

Web Sites

www.42explore.com/bully.htm

> This site has an extensive collection of links, activities and resources related to bullying.

www.antibullying.net

> A Scottish site based at the University of Edinburgh that offers ideas to teachers, parents and students about how to handle bullying.

www.bullying.co.uk

> This is a comprehensive British web site that has information for teachers, students and parents.

www.bullying.org

> This Canadian web site has information for adults about how to deal with and prevent bullying as well as stories, drawings and poems about kids' experiences with bullies.

www.bullypolice.org

> This is the web site of a watchdog organization that reports on state anti-bullying laws and provides resources for anti-bullying advocates.

www.cyberbully.org

> Developed by the Center for Safe and Responsible Internet Use, this site provides resources for educators and others to promote safe and responsible use of the internet. Offers a cyberbullying needs assessment survey that can be used by schools to gather information from students.

www.cyberbullying.org

> A Canadian web site that offers examples of cyberbullying, helpful resources, related articles from around the world, and practical strategies for both

preventing cyberbullying and dealing with it when it happens.

www.dontlaugh.org/

This is the web site of Operation Respect, a non-profit organization started by the folk singer Peter Yarrow to help organizations focused on children become more compassionate, safe and respectful environments. Operation Respect developed the Don't Laugh at Me character education programs for elementary- and middle-school students.

www.forkidsake.net

This contains a bullying survey that provides clear, uncomplicated answers to bullying issues that need to be addressed.

www.getnetwise.org

A public service by a wide range of Internet industry corporations and public interest organizations; its goal is for Internet users to be able to make informed decisions about their and their family's use of the Internet.

www.keystosaferschools.com/BullyingStopswhenRespect Begins.htm

This site dealing with school violence has a special section devoted to bullying.

www.kidshealth.org/teen/school_jobs/bullying/bullies.html

Advice for teens about dealing with bullying from TeensHealth.

www.lfcc.on.ca/bully.htm

This web page discusses at some length the practical issues involved in both responding to and preventing bullying incidents.

www.mentalhealth.samhsa.gov/15plus/aboutbullying.asp

This web page by the National Mental Health Information Center provides resources for both parents and educators about how to stop bullying.

www.nonamecallingweek.org

No Name-Calling Week is a week of educational activities held annually and intended to end name-calling in schools. The site also provides educators with the tools to lessen bullying in their communities.

www.principals.org/news/pl_hiddenworld_1202.cfm

This web page features the December 2002 issue of Principal Leadership magazine which focuses on "The Hidden World of Bullying."

www.stopbullyingnow.com

Offers practical research-based strategies and interventions to reduce bullying in schools.

www.stopbullyingnow.hrsa.gov

A site for both children and adults created by the U.S. Department of Health and Human Services as part of the Take a Stand. Lend a Hand. Stop Bullying Now! anti-bullying campaign.

www.teachers.net/gazette/MAR01/noll.html

Advice for parents and teachers on bullying from Kathy Noll, author of Taking the Bully by the Horns.

www.wiredsafety.org

Provides help, information, and education to Internet and cell phone users of all ages. Deals with cases of cyber-abuse, including identity and credential theft, online fraud, cyberstalking, hacking, and malicious code attacks.

Organizations

Atrium Society
PO Box 816
Middlebury, VT 05753
1-800-848-6021
www.atriumsoc.org

> This center offers educational services and materials
> that help children and adults to understand the roots
> of conflict, prejudice, nationalism and racism.

Center for Safe and Responsible Internet Use
474 West 29th Avenue
Eugene, OR 97405
541-344-9125
www.csriu.org

> Provides guidance to parents, educators, and others
> in ways that young people can use the Internet and
> other information technologies in a safe and respon-
> sible manner.

Educators for Social Responsibility
23 Garden Street
Cambridge, MA 02138
1- 617-492-1764
www.esrnational.org

> This organization helps educators create safe, caring,
> respectful, and productive learning environments.

I-SAFE America
5963 La Place Court, Suite 309
Carlsbad, CA 92008
1-760-603-7911
www.isafe.org

> A non-profit Internet foundation that promotes com-puter safety education and awareness to youth. Provides related age-appropriate K-12 curriculum to schools in all 50 states free of charge.

National Association of School Psychologists
4340 East West Highway, Suite 402
Bethesda, MD 20814
1-301-657-0270
www.nasponline.org

> This organization promotes educationally and psycho-logically healthy environments for children by imple-menting programs that prevent problems, foster independence and promote learning.

National Center for Assault Prevention
606 Delsea Drive
Sewell, NJ 08080
1-908-369-8972
www.ncap.org

> This organization offers training programs to help schools and communities prevent violence against children by teaching them practical skills and strate-gies. Offers a six-month bullying prevention program that includes workshops for staff, parents and students.

National School Safety Center
141 Duesenberg Drive, Suite 11
Westlake Village, CA 91362
1-805-373-9977
www.nssc1.org

Advocates for safe, secure and peaceful schools and identifies promising practices and programs that support safe schools for all students.

About the Author

Dr. Kenneth Shore

Dr. Kenneth Shore received his doctorate in psychology from Rutgers University in 1981. He was a psychologist for various New Jersey schools for over 25 years and now has a private practice offering evaluation, therapeutic and consulting services. In 2001 he was awarded the Peterson Prize by Rutgers University for "outstanding contributions to professional psychology" and in 2004 was named School Psychologist of the Year in New Jersey. He has written six books, including Special Kids Problem Solver: Ready-to-Use Interventions for Helping All Students with Academic, Behavioral and Physical Problems (Prentice Hall, 1998) and Elementary Teacher's Problem Solver: A Practical A to Z Guide for Managing Classroom Behavior Problems (Jossey-Bass, 2003). Dr. Shore has appeared on CNN as well as a PBS television series called Raising Kids and been interviewed on numerous radio programs. In addition to writing a column for the web site Education World, he is a consulting psychologist for the New Jersey Juvenile Justice Commission. He has served as a consultant to the New York City Board of Education and was instrumental in developing the New Jersey YM-YWHA camp for children with learning disabilities. Dr. Shore is available to provide workshops and presentations and can be reached by e-mail at **ShoreK@aol.com** or at his web site at **http://drkennethshore.NPRinc.com**.